HISTORIC BARRHEAD

HISTORIC SCOTLAND

HISTORIC BARRHEAD

Archaeology and development

E Patricia Dennison, Simon Stronach and Russel Coleman

THE SCOTTISH BURGH SURVEY

CBA
COUNCIL FOR BRITISH
ARCHAEOLOGY

THE UNIVERSITY OF EDINBURGH

East Renfrewshire
COUNCIL

Published by
The Council for British Archaeology and Historic Scotland.
First published in 2008

copyright © 2008 Historic Scotland
The moral right of the authors has been asserted.
British Library Cataloguing in Publication Data
A catalogue card for this book is available from the British Library

Edited by Catrina Appleby, CBA and Mark Watson, Historic Scotland
Page design and typesetting by Carnegie Publishing Ltd

Printing and Binding: The Alden Group
ISBN: 978-1-902771-69-4

Council for British Archaeology
St Mary's House
66 Bootham
York
YO30 7BZ
www.britarch.ac.uk

Historic Scotland
Longmore House
Salisbury Place
Edinburgh
EH9 1SH
Tel. 0131 668 8600
Fax. 0131 668 8669
www.historic-scotland.gov.uk

Front cover: Barrhead from the air looking north-west, 1953
(by courtesy of RCAHMS (RAF Air Photographs Collection) © Crown Copyright RCAHMS)
Insets: Barrhead in 1857, OS 1st edition map, 1:2500; Arthurlie Cross

Contents

Figures

Abbreviations

GUARD	Glasgow University Archaeological Research Division
NAS	National Archives of Scotland
NLS	National Library of Scotland
NMRS	National Monuments Record of Scotland
NSA	*The New Statistical Account of Scotland* (Edinburgh, 1834–45)
OSA	*The Statistical Account of Scotland 1791–99*, Sir John Sinclair (ed) New edition I R Grant and D J Withrington (eds) (Wakefield, 1978)
RCAHMS	Royal Commission on the Ancient and Historical Monuments of Scotland

Acknowledgements

Research for this Survey was undertaken by Headland Archaeology and the Centre for Scottish Urban History, University of Edinburgh in the spring of 2005. The authors would particularly like to express their gratitude to Dr Winifred Coutts and Sonia Baker for their research and great assistance in writing this Survey.

We are grateful for the support and assistance of a number of individuals and organisations. The library staff at Barrhead Community Library, East Renfrewshire Council were extremely helpful, as were the librarians at the Local History Library, Giffnock Library, East Renfrewshire Council, and the Mitchell Library, Glasgow. In Edinburgh, the National Library of Scotland staff and, in particular, the staff of the Map Library at Causewayside were consistently supportive. We would like also to thank the National Archives of Scotland and the Royal Commission on the Ancient and Historical Monuments of Scotland. The British Library kindly provided enlarged photocopies of General Roy's *Military Survey of Scotland* (1747–55).

We benefited from the advice of Stuart Jeffries of the West of Scotland Archaeology Service and of Richard Strachan of Historic Scotland. Nerys Tunnicliffe at Glasgow City Archives was very helpful. Particular thanks are due to Mrs Irene Hughson; Mrs Maud Devine, Local History Librarian, Giffnock Library, East Renfrewshire Council; Ms Julie Nichol of Planning and Regeneration, East Renfrewshire Council; Martin Brann and Mark Watson of Historic Scotland, all of whom agreed to read our script and made extremely useful comments. We would also like to thank colleagues at Edinburgh University for their helpful input on various points.

The Survey of Barrhead was funded by Historic Scotland. Historic Scotland acknowledges the generous contribution of East Renfrewshire Council towards the cost of publication.

1   Use of the Burgh Survey

The third series of Burgh Surveys is intended both as a guide for the general reader to research the rich history and archaeology of Scotland's burghs and to furnish local authorities with reliable information to help protect and manage the urban historic environment. This Survey provides a broad-ranging synthesis of existing knowledge about Barrhead, as well as highlighting research areas that would benefit from more detailed historical and archaeological analysis.

In its role as a tool for local authorities to use in the planning process, the first point of reference in this volume is the colour-coded town plan (**fig 35** and **broadsheet**) which depicts the areas of prime archaeological interest. The general index enables rapid access to information specific to a site, street or feature within the town.

Further information on the archaeological potential of a site or area within the town can be gleaned from local and national libraries and archives. The PASTMAP website (http://www.PASTMAP.org.uk) can also be consulted. This interactive website, supported jointly by Historic Scotland and the Royal Commission on the Ancient and Historical Monuments of Scotland, allows anyone to search data on Scotland's historic environment, including the legally protected sites – scheduled ancient monuments and listed buildings.

Both this Burgh Survey and the PASTMAP website provide information only. Where development is being considered, advice should in all cases be sought from the Local Authority planning department, and from their archaeological advisers: for East Renfrewshire, the West of Scotland Archaeology Service (Charing Cross Complex, 20 India Street, Glasgow, G2 4PF; telephone: 0141 287 8333) should be contacted.

2 Site and Setting

Introduction

Barrhead, in East Renfrewshire, lies across the valley of the Levern Water to the south-west of Glasgow at the base of the steep flanks of the Fereneze Hills. The town developed in the late eighteenth century as a consequence of the booming textile industry. Two factors about the location made it attractive for early industrialists, the most important of which was the Levern Water, which provided water for mills and bleachfields (**fig 1**). The town also benefited from being on an established route between Glasgow and Ayrshire (now the A736).

The settlement developed on the gentler southern bank of the Levern valley, along what is now Main Street. The area was not unoccupied before this development, although it has inevitably obscured the earlier settlements, chapels, and tower houses that once lined the valley. In the same way, more modern development has encroached on the weavers' cottages, mills, and

FIGURE I
Location map: Barrhead and surrounding area
(*Prepared by Headland Archaeology; based on OS mapping; © Crown copyright. All rights reserved. Historic Scotland Licence no. 100017509 [2008]*)

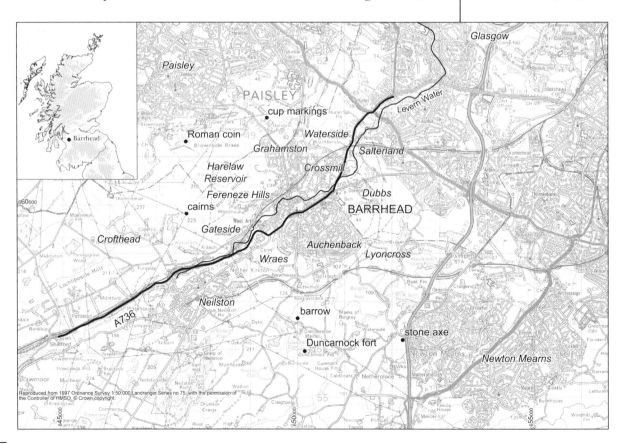

bleachfields of the nineteenth century (**figs 2 & 3**). The town's name derives from a combination of the Gaelic *barr* (summit) and the English *head*.[1]

Land use and geology

The Fereneze Hills are formed from hard basalt lavas while the town and undulating farmland to the east overlie sedimentary rocks which are mainly limestone.[2] These were laid down in the Carboniferous period (350 to 270 million years ago) when the area was covered with tropical forests.[3] Within the rocks, coal seams developed which have had a profound impact on the development of the town. The surrounding area also contains sandstone outcrops, which provided much of the building material for the nineteenth-century town.

The agricultural potential of the land around the town is somewhat limited by a tendency towards poorly draining clayey soils and a wet climate.[4] This

makes it most suited to grassland although a narrow range of crops (for example, barley, oats, and forage crops) can be grown with good management.[5] The uplands of the Fereneze Hills can be used only for grassland.

Economy

Prior to the town's development, the area would have been used predominantly for farming although the slopes of the Fereneze Hills seem to have been a popular hunting ground for members of the local gentry. In the later eighteenth century, the textile industry in the Scottish central belt was becoming industrialised and the town developed as part of the subsequent boom.

The banks of the Levern Water were an ideal location for cotton mills and bleachfields. A railway to the town from Glasgow was opened in 1848 and stoneware manufacture began shortly after. This endeavour was later to acquire a degree of fame for producing Shanks' sanitary ware.[6] As noted above, the town was close to a number of coal seams and these were exploited. An iron foundry and a quarry opened in the early twentieth century. Most recently, the town has expanded greatly with the construction of housing estates, from which many residents commute to Glasgow. The general decline in manufacturing industries over the last 30 years has affected Barrhead in common with many other central belt towns. However, its proximity to Paisley and Glasgow means it has the potential to take advantage of improving economic conditions.

Sources of evidence

This survey has examined a significant body of both primary and secondary source material, as may be noted in the endnotes and the bibliography. Time did not allow, however, an exhaustive trawl of all the potential documentation and suggested avenues of further research are noted in the final chapter.

Precious little archaeological interest has been expended on Barrhead and only one modern excavation has been undertaken in the town.[7] However, several authorities have commented on the Arthurlie Cross, a fine sculptured free-standing cross shaft (the head unfortunately having been lost), which now stands on Springhill Road (**fig 4**). The town is also known to be the location of several medieval sites such as the Tower of Rais and the Chapel of Ferm.

Historic maps, the earliest being a plan made by Timothy Pont around the end of the sixteenth century (**fig 6**), are a good source of information concerning the town's development. These can be consulted at the Map Library of the National Library of Scotland at Causewayside, Edinburgh, and many are available on their website.

The National Monuments Record of Scotland holds information relating to archaeological sites and chance finds in and around the town. This is accessible through their CANMORE database, which can be accessed through the internet. They also hold a collection of historic photographs and pictures relating to the town. The West of Scotland Archaeology Service, archaeological

FIGURE 3
Barrhead from the air, 1946 (106G/SCOT/UK 140, frame 5253), north at top, centred on Dovecothall and Shanks' factory.
(By courtesy of RCAHMS (RAF Air Photographs Collection);
© *Crown copyright RCAHMS)*

advisers to East Renfrewshire Council, also maintains a database of archaeological information. The National Archives of Scotland hold many historic plans relating to estates and engineering works; their catalogues can be accessed online. Last but not least, East Renfrewshire Council have created a Barrhead Heritage Trail and the accompanying blue plaques provide information relating to the town's past.

Listed buildings and scheduled ancient monuments

The Arthurlie Cross (**fig 4**) is designated as a scheduled ancient monument, meaning it has national importance and has been given statutory protection. Just outside the town, the fort of Duncarnock is also a scheduled ancient monument (**fig 1**).

Eighteen buildings or structures within or immediately around the town are protected as listed buildings: these range in nature from churches to stables. The list is maintained for the Scottish Ministers by Historic Scotland which assesses the structures and assigns each a category based on their importance. This status can be derived from historic or architectural merit, or a combination of the two. None of the listed structures in Barrhead is listed Category A (of national or international importance); eleven are listed as Category B (of regional importance); and six buildings are listed as Category C(S) (of local importance).

FIGURE 4
Arthurlie Cross, 2005

The archaeology of the area before the town developed

Prehistory

When settlers arrived in Scotland following the end of the last Ice Age, around 10,000 years ago, the landscape would have been heavily wooded and travel would have been easiest along river valleys.[8] It is likely that the area around the Clyde and its tributaries, such as the Levern Water, would have been settled from an early date. These Mesolithic (literally meaning Middle Stone Age) communities lived by hunting and gathering on land shared with deer, elk, aurochs, bear and boar. Around 4000 BC (the start of the Neolithic/New Stone Age), domesticated plants and animals were introduced, farming took hold and the land was gradually cleared.

The earliest recorded finds in the Barrhead area date from the Neolithic period and comprise a stone adze found in the town *c* 1950 and a stone axe found near Newton Mearns in 1938 (**fig 1**).[9] Some burial cairns found on top of the Fereneze Hills and some cup-markings on a rock between the town and Paisley (**fig 1**) may date to the same period or, perhaps more likely, to the subsequent Bronze Age.[10] Early accounts also tell of the discovery of 'several urns with bones in them, surrounded with square free-stones' in the vicinity and it is likely these are Bronze Age cremation burials within cists.[11]

By the start of the Iron Age in Scotland, *c* 600 BC, the landscape is likely to have been heavily settled and fortifications became more common. One such appears to have been nearby Duncarnock Fort, to the south of the town (**fig 1**). Sited on a rocky knoll, a 10 ft (3 m) thick wall encircles an area *c* 190 m x 100 m. Fragments of Iron Age pottery and worked shale have been found within the defences and the fort is protected as a scheduled ancient monument.[12] It has been suggested that the fort was also occupied in the early historic period, although there is little evidence to support this.[13]

Roman period

When the Romans invaded they described the area as occupied by a tribe called the *Damnonii*.[14] The first significant military incursions into Scotland were led by the governor Agricola *c* AD 80.[15] Little is known about these and within about twenty years all his conquests had been lost.[16] It was not until AD 142, under the rule of the Emperor Antoninus Pius (AD 138–61), that the famous wall was built to the north of the Clyde. Presumably by that time the area lay under Roman control but it is not thought to have been close to any forts or roads.[17] Consequently, it is probable that the inhabitants of the Levern Water valley had little or no contact with the Romans, who were likely to have concentrated on maintaining their communication network and ensuring a friendly local aristocracy rather than neighbourhood policing.[18] The only trace of the Romans' presence that has been discovered around the town was a coin found to the north-west (**fig 1**). The Antonine Wall and its forts were abandoned *c* AD 160 and the formal boundary of the empire moved to Hadrian's Wall, far to the south.

Notes

1   M Darton, *The Dictionary of Place Names in Scotland* (Orpington, 1994), 164

2   Soil Survey of Scotland, *South- West Scotland Soil*, 1:250,000 scale, Sheet 6 (Aberdeen, 1982); Institute of Geological Sciences, *The Limestones of Scotland* (Edinburgh, 1976), 160

3   J Gifford and F A Walker (eds), *The Buildings of Scotland: Stirling and Central Scotland* (London, 2002), 3

4   Soil Survey of Scotland, *South-West Scotland Land Capability for Agriculture*, 1:250,000 Sheet 6 (Aberdeen, 1982)

5   *Ibid*

6   R Smith, *The Making of Scotland* (Edinburgh, 2001), 82

7   M Donnelly, 'Levern Walkway, Barrhead, East Renfrewshire' (unpublished GUARD report, 1999)

8   J N G Ritchie, 'Prehistoric and Early Historic Stirling and Central Scotland', in Gifford and Walker (eds), *Buildings of Scotland,* 9–11

9   *NMRS Record nos* NS55NW 15; NS55NW 2

10   *NMRS Record nos* NS45NE 19; NS46SE 39

11   *OSA*, xiii, 148

12   *NMRS Record no* NS55NW 3

13   L R Laing, *The Archaeology of late Celtic Britain and Ireland c 400–1200 AD* (London, 1975)

14   T Darvill, *Prehistoric Britain* (London, 1987), 181

15   D J Breeze, ' The Romans in Stirling and Central Scotland', in Gifford and Walker (eds), *Buildings of Scotland,* 12

16   W S Hanson, *Agricola and the Conquest of the North* (London, 1987), 150

17   Ordnance Survey, *Map of Roman Britain* (4th edn, 1978)

18   Hanson, *Agricola and the Conquest of the North*, 173

3 History and archaeology

Sites and locations mentioned in this chapter are shown in **fig 34**.

Introduction

Barrhead is a settlement that succeeded by dint of its position and natural resources – it was in the right place at the right time. The right place was the west of Scotland, close to Glasgow and Paisley, the right time was the end of the eighteenth century, and the natural resource in abundance was the Levern Water and its tributaries. These were essential for printing and bleaching, and to run water-powered textile machines. The growth of Barrhead began with rural proto-industry and took off with the rise of eighteenth- and nineteenth-century manufacturing industries.[1] Its elevation to a burgh in 1893 merely confirmed its status. The burgh's later development followed the general trends in British industry, and much of 'old' Barrhead was swept away with road widening and factory clearance schemes in the twentieth century. With the closure of the Shanks factory site in 1992, Barrhead was identified as a priority for action. The former Renfrew District Council and its successor, East Renfrewshire Council, have worked to make the town an attractive place for people to live and work with the support of the European Regional Development Fund. Most recently, a major regeneration strategy was approved by East Renfrewshire Council in 2006. Part of this will seek to reintroduce industry back into Barrhead by creating attractive, highly accessible business sites. Barrhead is also included in the recently published 'Scottish Small Towns report 2007–2013', which is seeking to showcase the plight of this often missed sector of Scottish life.

The early historic and medieval periods

Following the departure of the Romans, the Barrhead area lay somewhere between the ill-defined territories held, and frequently fought over, by the Britons, Scots, Angles, and Picts in central Scotland.[2] It seems most likely that for much of the time the town lay within the kingdom of Strathclyde, which had its capital at Dumbarton Rock. A link to an early ecclesiastical centre at Govan is certainly suggested by the form of the Arthurlie cross-shaft (**fig 4**).[3] This sculpture, the earliest standing monument in Barrhead, is likely to date from the tenth or early eleventh century,[4] when the Scots and Picts were forming an alliance that was the genesis of the medieval Scottish kingdom.

Although now lacking its head, the shaft still stands 2.2m high, is impressively carved and shows the influence of a variety of styles.[5] The cross shaft is very worn on one side but on the other a distinctive 'buried cross' motif can be seen; the other faces are decorated with fine knotwork.[6] Stylistically, it has been compared to the well-known group of crosses from Govan.[7] Now erected on Springhill Road, the shaft is not in its original position. The first *Statistical Account* of the parish in 1791 states that at that time it was being used as a footbridge over a stream that divided the grounds of Arthurlie from those of Hawkshead.[8] Plans of the lands of Hawkshead make it clear that this stream was the Kirkton Burn.[9] It is recorded that the cross was rediscovered *c* 1831 in Colinbar Glen, through which the Kirkton Burn runs.[10] It was subsequently erected in the grounds of Arthurlie House, until *c* 1942 when it was moved by Barrhead Council to its present location (NS 4997 5854), at the junction of Carnock Crescent and Springfield Road.

Presumably this large, and heavy, monument would not have been moved far from its original site to be used as a footbridge. It may be relevant that part of the town is still known as Cross Arthurlie, and that the meeting of roads this referred to lay at the foot of Colinbar Glen. It is also possible that the name derived from the original location of the Arthurlie Cross. There is evidence that suggests there may have been at least one other example in the area. When John Ainslie surveyed the town in 1796, he marked a 'Corse Stane' (presumably 'Cross Stone'), close to the road as it leaves the town to the south-west (**fig 5**). Since it is known from historical accounts that by this time the Arthurlie Cross was being used as a bridge over the Kirkton Burn, it would seem that this must be another, previously unrecorded, stone cross.

Free-standing stone crosses are usually connected with ecclesiastic or church sites in the early medieval period. A single example would suggest that such a site is possible in the Barrhead area; the presence of two stone crosses makes it more likely. In this context crosses are often used to mark the boundary of church lands, as was the case with the girth cross that formerly stood outside Holyrood Abbey at the foot of the Royal Mile in Canongate, Edinburgh. It is possible that an early church site included the holy well of St Connel (NGR NS 4930 5886) and developed into the Chapel of Ferm (**fig 34**). Certainly the dedication to St Connel is interesting: the name is variously spelled, and is known locally as 'Conval', but seems to be derived from a seventh-century Irish saint and follower of Glasgow's St Mungo.[11] It is chronicled that he was a missionary who worked south of the Clyde.[12] However, it should be noted that both crosses appear to have been located on the south side of the Levern Water and this offers an alternative location for the possible early Christian site with which they were once associated.

It is possible to state with certainty that the medieval Chapel of Ferm was located in the vicinity of Chappell House (**fig 34**). The chapel is shown on Pont's map of the late sixteenth century, where it is labelled the 'Chapel of Fermm' (**fig 6**).[13] A lazar house or hospital under the control of Paisley Abbey

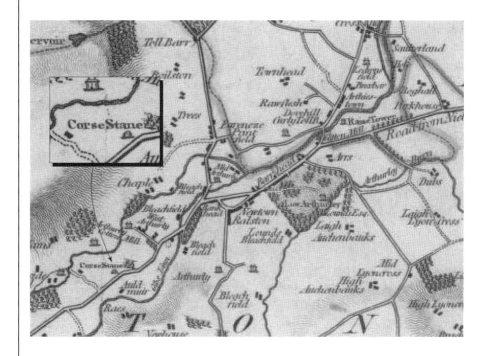

was said to be located at Chappell.[14] There certainly seems to have been a hospital situated beside the Levern Water somewhere between Neilston and Crookston but there is no evidence to suggest it was necessarily at Barrhead.[15] Little else is known of it other than that it has been claimed that the chapel was in decline by 1450.[16] The dedication appears to have been to St Connel, and a drystone masonry well (see above) that also carries this dedication survives to this day. Maps confirm that the chapel had been removed by the late eighteenth century. A fine villa and stable block, built in the second half of the eighteenth century, now occupy the site which is on a level terrace with a steep drop to the Levern Water.[17] According to the current owner of the villa, the basement of the house is on a different alignment and extends beyond the standing exterior walls. Although difficult to say without physical examination, it is possible that this originated as part of an earlier building, perhaps even the chapel itself.

In 1160, Robert de Croc of Crocstoun assigned the patronage of Neilstoun to the monks of the Abbey of Paisley, in return for a regular mass said for the benefit of his soul.[18] Robert de Croc's heiress married Stewart of Darnly [sic], giving rise to the Lennox and Darnley line.[19] The lordship of Neilston passed by marriage to Cunningham of Craigends;[20] later still it was divided between several owners.

Several interesting sites are known to have occupied the area in the medieval period. The most accurately located is that known as the Tower of Rais, and later as Stewart's Rais, in the north-east of the town (**fig 34**). The name 'Rais' was first recorded in the thirteenth century and it seems likely that

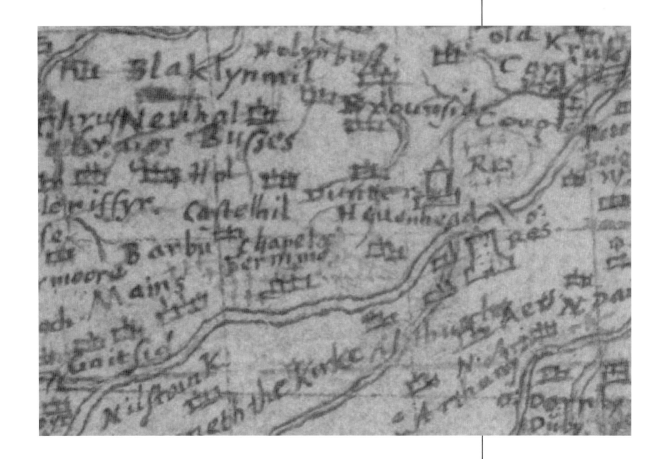

FIGURE 6
Timothy Pont's map of
the Barrhead area, from
Renfrewshire, c 1590s
(Reproduced by permission of
the Trustees of the National
Library of Scotland)

some form of defensive structure was present by this time.[21] This structure seems to have been replaced by the Darnley family with a tower, built as a hunting residence between 1437 and 1449, that stood until the beginning of the twentieth century.[22] It was a square structure of several storeys and is likely to have been accompanied by ancillary buildings such as stables. An excavation before the construction of a cycle route in 1999 exposed a corner of the tower's foundations.[23] The excavations suggested that the building may have been accompanied by a smithy.[24]

The earliest depiction of the tower is on the map created by Timothy Pont towards the end of the sixteenth century (**fig 6**). This shows the tower as a large building, interestingly labelled 'O Res', with the 'O' probably meaning 'Over'. A little way to the north is what appears to be a bridge over the Levern Water. It is possible that Pont could have intended the markings to represent a ford, but the definition is such that the probability is that it is a bridge. On the other side of the river, another tower is also marked 'Res'. The exact location of the latter is not now known. These towers seem likely to have guarded both sides of this crossing over the Levern Water, at least when such defences were considered necessary. Blaeu produced an attractive representation in 1654 (**fig 8**), although this was based on Pont's earlier plan. By the time of

Ainslie's plan of 1796 (**fig 5**), only the tower on the south side of the Levern Water is depicted, the other presumably having been demolished.

It is said that at one time the tower was used to house a beam engine to pump water from a nearby coal mine.[25] In any event, it was recorded in 1831 that almost all of the structure had gone, with the stone carted off for local buildings (**fig 9**).[26] Perhaps these included the farmhouse at Dubbs (**fig 1**), where it was recorded in the 1970s that stones from the tower were included in the farm buildings.[27]

By the time of Alexander III (1249–86), the lands of the Levern and the area round Crookston were more settled. Fords crossed the river, a ford at Dovecothall reportedly being still in use at the end of the nineteenth century.[28] From written documents and Pont's early plan (**fig 6**), it seems clear that the modern town spread over several small settlements that probably originated in the medieval period; a number are associated with the name 'Arthurlie', of which there appear to be three on early maps (**fig 8**). In 1452, Arthurlie passed to the Darnley family.[29] In this period, Arthurley appears to be the main name for the area that later became known as Barrhead. Other small farming settlements or fermtouns seem to have been located at Aurs (Aers), Auchenback (Ackinbae), Beneth the Kirke, Duby (Dubbs), Chapel of Fermane (Fereneze), and Lyocors (Lyoncross). These remain distinct at the time of the first Ordnance Survey plan of the area in the mid-nineteenth century (**fig 10**) and it is possible to locate them fairly accurately in relation to the modern town (**fig 1**).

Some authors have suggested that there was another small settlement to the north, in the Dovecothall area.[30] This is asserted to have been present from the thirteenth century and was originally called 'Ducatmyllne'. This is not clearly identifiable on Pont's map although there is certainly settlement in the area by the time of Ainslie's survey in 1796 (**fig 5**).

It should be noted that Main Street and the A736 are likely to follow a route that was established by the medieval period, if not earlier. This would seem to have included in all probability a bridge, but possibly a ford, over the Levern Water at Bridgebar (*c* 1 km to the north-east) by the late sixteenth century when Pont made his plan (**fig 6**).

Outside the town, but also of note, is Wraes Mill *c* 1 km to the south-west (**fig 7**). This was recorded by Pont and may well be medieval in origin. A nineteenth-century mill still survives there (Category C(S)-listed), now converted to a house. It was one of the eight mill sites noted to have stood on the Levern Water in the medieval and post-medieval period.[31]

The seventeenth century

The small settlements of Dovecothall, Aurs, Arthurlie, Fereneze, and Dealston are all thought to have been in existence at the beginning of the seventeenth century (**fig 8**).[32] For many years Barrhead was merely part of the parish of Neilston, Renfrewshire. Like many other people all over Renfrewshire, those in Neilston supported the Covenanters, in *c* 1672 apparently travelling from Dovecothall, Lyoncross, and Arthurlie to worship at Mearns Castle, some 6 km to the south-east.[33] It has been suggested that the population at the time of the 1695 poll tax, in the area that was later covered by Barrhead burgh, was between 300 and 400; most worked on the land, and only 21 were weavers.[34]

The eighteenth century

William Roy's *Military Survey*[35] of the mid-eighteenth century focused on the access routes through the countryside, depicting roads, bridges, and the locations of the scattered fermtouns. Bridgebarr appears in the present-day Dovecothall location, and Dunterly is south-east of Fereneze mill. There are four settlements called Arthurly [sic] – just one is designated as 'E Arthurley'. Achinback appears twice, both located south-east of Dubbs.

Beginnings of a community

Barrhead grew rapidly from the modest settlements where handloom weavers lived when it suddenly had to accommodate large bleachfields and spinning mills. While every village had its own community of weavers, it seems that the

FIGURE 7
Wraes Mill with miller's house in background, 1965 *(By courtesy of RCAHMS; © Crown copyright RCAHMS).*

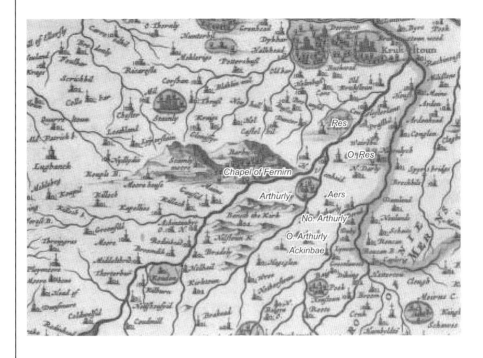

Res

O. Res

Chapel of Fernirn

Arthurly

Aers

No. Arthurly

O. Arthurly

Ackinbae

FIGURE 8
Detail from J Blaeu's *The
Baronie of Renfrow*, 1654
*(Reproduced by permission of
the Trustees of the National
Library of Scotland)*

weavers were drawn to Newtown Ralston, particularly around the later Cloth Street area.[36] While it is unclear exactly when it was built, the 'new town' village of Ralston (later called Craigheads) was the work of Gavin Ralston, who built the workers' tenements here after he married into the local Pollock family in 1780.[37] By this time, 'in Newton-Ralston, Barrhead, Dovecothall and Grahamston, there are about seventy weavers' houses, containing about 130 looms … the four places lying contiguous to one another [along the] Levern [and the] Kirkton'.[38] The weavers' houses accommodated the loom on the ground floor, and the family home upstairs.

It has been suggested[39] that the main part of Barrhead originally ran between Foundry Brae and Water Road, with the latter being the oldest street in the area; there is a long history of schools on the site, the last of the buildings here being demolished in 1968. The site of an early weaver's cottage is thought to have stood opposite Water Road, on Lowdnes' land, but there are no extant remains.[40]

While few buildings survive from this time, the property known as Trees (now the Fereneze Golf Clubhouse), and Chappell House and its stable block, are notable exceptions. The three-storey Trees possibly dates to *c* 1760. Chappell House is thought to date from *c* 1800, and is probably built round an earlier building of *c* 1757; its stable block is also thought to be of this earlier date. It is possibly on the former site of the old chapel and hospital. All these buildings are listed Category B (**fig 34**).

It is clear that Levernside folk were determined to go their own way in the matter of belief. From 1738, the Secession movement attracted a lot

FIGURE 9
Stewart's Rais Tower, from
C Taylor, *Levern Delineated...*
(Glasgow, 1831)
*(By courtesy of the Mitchell
Library, Glasgow)*

of local support, with worshippers happy to walk to Glasgow to follow their beliefs. When the Glasgow Secession Church itself split in 1747, the residents of western Neilston followed the Burghers, taking their worship to Pollokshaws.[41] Following a petition from 347 residents, Barrhead got its own Secession (Burgher) congregation on 5 March 1793;[42] it used a hall in Nailer's Row, near Glen Street, until its own church opened in 1796.[43] This was located where the modern health and sports centres are on the north side of Main Street.

Population

Renfrewshire saw by far the biggest population increase of any Scottish county in the second half of the eighteenth century. Barrhead itself is mentioned just a few times in the *Statistical Account* written in 1797, although it seems to have existed from *c* 1750; nonetheless, the description of life in Neilston parish was clearly relevant to the area in general. There were 439 people living in the village of Barrhead, nearly nineteen per cent of a total parish population of 2330.[44] This was nearly as many as lived in Neilston (472), and more evidently lived in the settlements of Dealston, Fereneze, West Arthurlie, Ralston, Arthurlie, Aurs, and Dovecothall, which all lay in the vicinity of Barrhead and Neilston.[45]

Transport

As regards transport,[46] it seems that a road running from Dovecothall, over the river near Rais Tower (**fig 9**) and up the hill to Water Road in the old heart of the village, linked these settlements; the road/lane continued through what later became Muriel Street, onto Blackbyres and beyond. Water Road itself followed the Levern to Foundry Brae, then Kirkton Burn to Bourock, and through the houses called Salt Lakes; from here one road went up Kelburn Street to West Arthurlie, the other past Kirkton. Another source mentions merely that the principal route ran from Kelburn Street to Chapelbrae, at Dovecothall, with a second route from Cross Arthurlie Street to Cross-Stobs along the Paisley Road.[47]

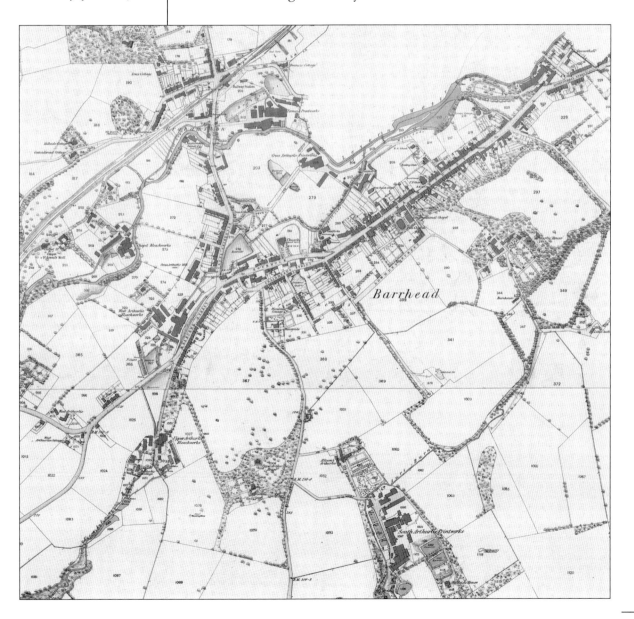

From the mid-eighteenth century, the new Turnpike Act meant that roads were improved. By 1770 one road went from Pollokshaws, Dovecothall, and Neilston to Stewarton; another from Aurs to Mearns. Tolls were collected at Dovecothall, at Bridgebar.[48] A fairly reliable source, however, describes the roads in the 1790s as 'of a very impassable kind, and the usual mode of conveyance for goods was by packhorse'.[49] Nonetheless, an eighteenth-century road bridge (Category C(S)-listed) over the Levern Water (NS 512 602) survives at Salterland (**figs 1 & 17**), described as having 'two segmental arches ... rubble built with squared voussoirs, pointed cutwaters, [and] ashlar coping'.[50]

Manufactures: textiles

The earliest of all the manufactures in Barrhead village was weaving; by 1792 there were 85 looms, which were 'mostly employed in working muslin, and silk-gauze. A few in what is called county work (linen etc) for private families'[51] (**fig 11**).

It seems that all the Levern valley settlements accommodated handloom weavers. This industry was expanding right across lowland Scotland, but the Levern villages were different because of their proximity to both Glasgow and Paisley and because of the establishment of print and bleachfields in the area. High-value, high-quality, fine weaving marks Renfrewshire out as different from the rest of Scotland. However, the number of villages given over solely to weaving was small compared to the size of Paisley, so the impetus for the industrial revolution here lies rather in the extensive bleach and print fields, and then the cotton spinning mills, that used the water in the area in the later eighteenth century.

Weavers during this and earlier periods worked as a family unit, untroubled by set times and production levels. The wife would spin and wind pirns,

FIGURE 11
Possible weaver's cottage to right, Main Street, 2005

and the husband would weave, their children assisting where they could. Most people would also work a small plot of land, and spinning and weaving were fitted round other work. By the end of the century there had been a move from subsistence agriculture with some weaving, through subsistence weaving, supplemented by some agriculture, to full-time weaving or bleaching. Handloom weaving continued to be important as a male occupation, alongside new activities that were developing for other members of the family. Once spinning was mechanised it was de-skilled, much of the work being done by migrant workers, both adults and children, from the rural Lowlands, the Highlands and Ireland.[52] The amount of yarn produced increased enormously, making more work for weavers, and the work itself was managed so that the weavers were essentially outworkers for merchant manufacturers.

In 1792, there was some discussion between the manufacturers as to the way business was likely to go; the 'silk-gauze trade', in decline in the recent past, was 'reviving', and it was thought that it might exceed apparently the cotton business. Others, however, felt that the cotton trade was ripe for expansion.[53] Lancashire workers moved to the Levern area, and the Scots were able to benefit from their experience. Building on the back of existing Scottish skills in the production of linens and silk, they concentrated on fine cottons, that is, cotton yarn, cambrics, and muslins.[54]

The following description in the Old Statistical Account makes clear why the lands along the waters of the parish were so valued. The Levern Water runs south-west to north-east, passing Gateside, West Arthurlie, Fereneze, Chappell, and Dovecothall.[55]

The Lavern-water … is naturally small; but within these few years, some companies concerned in the cotton-mill, the Faraneze print-field and several bleachfields[56] situated along its banks … obtained a lease with liberty to get the source of this water dammed up, with a breast-work about 16 feet high. The springs above this … [are] numerous … [even] during the greatest drought in summer … there is [a] plentiful supply of water to drive all the machinery in the public works erected and still erecting on this stream.[57]

and,

There are several other rivulets in this parish, which, from the vicinitude to the large manufacturing towns of Glasgow and Paisley … have become of great value to the proprietors; all of them having their banks occupied with extensive bleachfields, which, in consequence of the excellent springs in their neighbourhood, (the purity of whose water is very great), and plenty of coals in this, and the adjoining parish of Paisley, carry on a most extensive business in bleaching, but chiefly of light goods as muslins, cambricks, lawns etc.[58]

Print and bleachfields

The start of the transformation of Neilston into a manufacturing parish has been dated to decisions taken in 1767–68.[59] The printing of calicoes began at Fereneze in 1773, at Boyd's Field, the property owner being A Graham, and this was for a long while the only printfield in the parish.[60] Roy's map shows just one mill: at Ferzeneze [sic].[61] The Reverend Henry Miller supposedly began an inkle[62] factory around this time, but the location is unknown as it would not have required water power. Printworks required some water power, but more was required for washing processes, drawn from clean sources rather than main rivers.

Bleachfields were more numerous, and there are differing views on which was the first established on the Levern. Some argue that it was established by an Irish bleacher, Peter Adair, at Cross Arthurlie c 1773,[63] but another source states that the location was West Arthurlie.[64] Others date the first to 1765 and locate this 'almost opposite where the Methodist Church now stands'.[65] Elsewhere, it is said that Graham of Chappell began a bleachfield at Fereneze, but this is not dated.[66] More fields followed (seven by 1782) and by 1837 there was an equal number of bleachfields and printfields. There is therefore a need to relate the historical accounts to specific sites. The bleachfields located on the slopes above the river Levern employed substantial numbers of people, and are the main reason for the growth of the town.

FIGURE 12

Dovecothall, Levern Mill, from C Taylor, *Levern Delineated…* (Glasgow, 1831) (*By courtesy of the Mitchell Library, Glasgow*)

Cotton spinning

Scotland was quick to follow the first water-powered cotton mills in Derbyshire, initially by breaking patents. Penicuik (1778), Rothesay (1779), Dovecothall and Busby Mills (1780), and Johnstone Mill (1782), relied on industrial espionage as they preceded Richard Arkwright's visit to Scotland in 1784 and his first licensed mills.[67]

It is of note that when Sir John Sinclair was selecting his 'specimen' parishes for the *Statistical Account*, in his efforts to 'sell' the notion elsewhere, he chose Neilston as his example of a newly industrialised parish. The mill at Dovecothall, Neilston parish, was the third established in Scotland, in 1778,[68] and was located where the old corn mill had been. In the parish as a whole there were 'two cotton mills ... two more erecting ... one large printfield, and 12 bleachfields'.[69] Both cotton mills were near Barrhead village.

The cotton mill at Dovecothall (**fig 12**), was built in 1780[70] and was '76 feet long, 28 feet wide, and 3 stories [sic] high'.[71] Some remains of the Levern Mill opposite can still be seen, accompanied by an explanatory noticeboard. The second cotton mill, built in 1786, was at Gateside,[72] and was '100 feet long, 31 feet wide and 2 stories [sic] high',[73] although Sinclair notes:

it is proposed to turn the whole of the latter into lodgings for the work people, and to erect a new mill on a much larger scale. The number of workmen [sic] employed in both mills is as follows:

Males above 15	29
Females above 15	100
Males under 15	94
Females under 15	78

Average of wages paid to the above work-people per month £217 or £2821 per annum.[74]

One of the cotton mills 'now erecting', that of Stewart, Orr & Company, was at Crofthead, just outside Neilston village, south of Gateside. Built in 1792, it was:

98 feet long, 34 feet wide and is being raised to 5 stories [sic] high; and will probably add 500 people to this parish. They will labour, however, under the disadvantage of not having a village in which to lodge their work-people, and must necessarily be put to great additional expence [sic] in buildings.[75]

Other mills came: Broadlie, near Neilston in 1790; West Arthurlie in 1790;[76] Crofthead (described above) in 1792, Levern, 1798, and finally in

FIGURE 13
Sluice gate near the site of
West Arthurlie bleachworks
(site 8 on Fig 34), 2005
(Headland Archaeology)

1801, that at Fereneze belonging to Mr Graham.[77] Graham had opened the first printfield in the area back in 1773,[78] and mills and printfields usually developed in tandem. At the far north-east end of the Levern was located the Corse Mill (c 1770).[79]

Large-scale cotton processing meant that each stage was broken down into its smaller steps, and large numbers of workers were required. Some would be skilled, but most were unskilled; women and children were ideal workers for Arkwright's water frame, and its successor the throstle, producing warp yarn. Other lighter tasks remained 'female/children's work', including the jobs of piecers and scavengers. Crompton's mule, best suited to producing weft yarn, needed male strength to return the carriage to its starting point.[81] Influence and power lay with the male mule spinner, in charge of his workers well into the following century.

Power-loom weaving seems to have been limited in the area to the existing spinning mills (such as Broadlie) and the sole purpose-built Cross Arthurlie Mill, which was recorded by Paisley Museum in 1982.

Of the six spinning mill sites in Neilston parish, those at Broadlie and Crofthead retain mill buildings from the mid and late 19th century, standing adjacent to the eighteenth-century water-powered sites. Gateside and West Arthurlie Mills have archaeological potential as their sites have not been subsequently developed. Some standing buildings and a wheel arch exist at the latter. Fereneze and Dovecothall Mills have been redeveloped. Some remnants can be seen associated with Levern Mill. A sluice gate which survives near the West Arthurlie bleachworks is another rare upstanding remnant (**fig 13**).

a

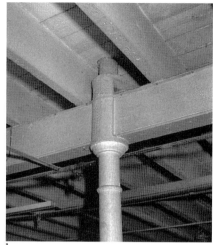

b

FIGURES 14
Fereneze Mills,
Barrhead, 1990
(a) Old Mill *c* 1801, extended
to right of downpipe in 1824,
with (b) typical column and
cylindrical saddle;
(c) New Mill, *c* 1830, with
(d) typical column and
square saddle *(all by courtesy
of RCAHMS; © Crown
copyright RCAHMS)*

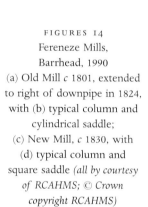

c

d

FIGURES 15
The Waterproofing Co
Works, Fereneze Mills,
Barrhead, *c* 1900.
The Old Mill is to the right
of the New Mill
*(© Crown copyright RCAHMS,
by courtesy of Mr T Thomson,
Fereneze Industrial Estate)*

Fereneze Mills burned down in May 1990 (**figs 14, 15 & 18**); just prior to that they were inspected by Mark Watson and his notes on the structures surviving at that time are included here. The buildings comprised two parallel ranges of stone-built mills. The first, begun in 1798 as a flax-spinning mill, was converted to cotton in 1801–03 after a fire (**fig 14a**).[80] It had an external circular brick stair tower (comparable to Murray's Mill, Manchester, 1798, and that at Broadlie Mill). The western portion of the mill was subsequently demolished and the east end extended by thirteen bays in 1824 (when the mill was increased by two-thirds, according to Factory Commission returns). The first mill was five storeys with floor to ceiling heights reducing floor to floor, from 10' (*c* 3 m), to 9' 9" to 8' 9" (*c* 2.6 m) to 8' (*c* 2.4 m) to 7' 2" (*c* 2.2 m). The six bays of the 1798/1801 part had a new steel structure inserted but the 1824 part retained its off-centre row of cast-iron columns of 3½" (89 mm) diameter. The columns on the lower floors had cylindrical saddles to transfer loads from floor to floor without crushing the timber beams that threaded through them (**fig 14b**). These were of the same type as those noted in an extension of 1825 to Cartside Mill, Kilbarchan, suggesting the same millwright was using products from one foundry.

A second mill, built south of the first, appeared to date from the 1820s or 1830s (**fig 14c**), and was probably a mule mill to provide weft yarn, requiring less power than the earlier mill; typically they came in pairs. On the west gable a flat-roofed building, probably a beam engine house, and an external hoist and stack of earth closets served each floor. A pilastered doorpiece faced into the yard. Square saddles at the column capitals suggested a slightly later construction than the extension to the first mill (**fig 14d**).

A three-storey wing connected the two mills at the west and a detached two-storey building at the east enclosed the yard. The latter may have performed ancillary functions such as bale opening, cotton warehouse, and counting house. Several brick buildings were subsequently added for use as a cloth waterproofing works.

In 1830 a new wheel, 12' by 24' (*c* 3.6m x 7.3m) diameter, was installed in a detached wheelhouse, a piend-roofed building by the later railway line, and gave 35 horsepower. This was a smaller version of similar detached wheelhouses at Catrine, Ayrshire, Deanston and Stanley Mills, Perthshire of the 1820s. A turbine was subsequently placed there. The small beam engine house at the second mill shows reliance on hybrid power sources as water could not be relied upon alone.

Arches over the tail race underlay both mills, and the arch carrying the later railway line indicates its route into the complex

Housing the workers

The new industries needed a local labour force and by the 1780s the Earl of Glasgow was creating plots of land alongside the road to Neilston, which later became Main Street. The place name 'Barrhead' appears for the first time on Ainslie's plan of 1796 (**fig 5**) and development seems to have been concentrated on the south side of the road (**fig 3**). Manufacturing demanded water, both as a source of power and as a necessary part of the processing. Accessible raw materials and, above all, access to a workforce were also essential; the latter was generally lacking in rural areas. At New Lanark, this problem was overcome by providing accommodation in a purpose-built village close to the mill. At Barrhead, the Printers' Row tenement was an example of the houses built for the Highland workers at the eastern end of the valley;[82] others were built at Upper Graham Street for the Fereneze workers,[83] and at Stewart Street, Dovecothall, for the Levern Mill workers. Mill villages were built at West Arthurlie[84] and at Newton Ralston (Craigheads); foremen's houses were erected at Upper Craigheads.[85]

In Neilston parish, it seems that some workers and their families were absorbed into existing villages, like Barrhead, while what were evidently single or widowed female migrant workers resided in:

> women-houses, so-called, erected on purpose near almost every field, where they lodge only during the working season, repairing to the neighbouring towns during the winter months, and perhaps not returning again to the same fields. This migratory class, in number 93, lodge at present in 7 women-houses …[86]

Employed at bleaching and drying goods, these 93 women – some of them under fifteen – were unskilled workers. One 'women-house' was apparently still in operation 'within living memory'[87] at Netherplace bleachfield in Mearns parish.

Principal among the buildings to survive from this period are large villas on the outskirts of town which have escaped redevelopment. A good example is Arthurlie House (**fig 16**), a fine villa built in 1780 and bought in 1818 by the master of Levern Mill.[88] These handsome structures and their gardens were a conspicuous display of the money being made by some sections of society from their investment in the new factories. Some of the stone for the building of Arthurlie House came from a vault elsewhere on the estate which was said to contain a skeleton.[89] Other buildings of note are Fereneze Golf Clubhouse which was probably built c 1760 and was formerly known as Trees, and Chappell House mentioned above.[90]

These airy, detached villas contrast with the small group of surviving buildings on the south side of Main Street. These nineteenth-century tenements and shops give context to the much rarer single-storey weavers' cottages that preceded them (**figs 11 & 30**).

FIGURE 16
Arthurlie House, 2005
(*Headland Archaeology*)

Those employed at the 'public works' were highly paid – nineteen shillings a week – compared with the ordinary workman's wage of one shilling and sixpence a day and with the male farm servant who received ten pounds sterling a year.[91] The attraction of employment in the new industries is clear.

Life in Barrhead

Accommodating workers away from existing centres of population raised a further problem: they were located away from the controlling aegis of the parish minister. In Barrhead's case, there was no Church of Scotland until the Chapel of Ease was built in 1840.[92]

Concern was expressed by the Neilston minister that:

the rapid increase of manufactures, is neither friendly to the health, nor morals of the people. In cotton mills a multitude of children are employed before they even receive common education. They therefore spend perhaps a considerable part of their life, without any other principles for the direction of their conduct, but those which natural conscience dictates. The lower ranks of mankind, however, when collected and confined together, are too apt to corrupt one another; and when assembled in such promiscuous crowds, are probably exposed not to the best example … The children too, in these works, confined as it were, to the very point of a spindle, must of course have narrow ideas and contracted minds. [93]

It was also noted that the proposal that some education be provided had been partially accepted, but that the suggestion that children should not be employed until they had some education was 'disregarded'. Having dealt with the moral aspect of the working environment, the author continued:

The finer parts of the cotton, also, in the progress of the work, flying off continually by friction, fills the atmosphere in which they breathe, with unwholesome particles, and it is probably from this cause that their appearance is so pale and sickly.[94]

The concern seemed not to be for the health of the people themselves, but for the health of the government's military recruits. By the 1790s, there was increasing anxiety that Britain was no longer the invincible military force it once was. Following the outbreak of war with France in 1793, the questions asked of the contributors to the *Statistical Account* of the 1790s reflected the concerns of the time.

The nineteenth century

Transport

Between 1790 and 1828 it was said that 'villages have sprung up in the vicinity of every public work and the roads have become equal to those in any part of the kingdom'.[95] In 1820, the village was connected to Irvine and Glasgow by its third turnpike road;[96] an 'almost level', 'splendid' turnpike road, complete with a number of bridges.[97] A good transport service was provided between Irvine and Glasgow by four stagecoaches, with the Levern Inn as a staging-house.[98]

A railway was deemed to be required to more easily transport the coal necessary for powering the manufactures.[99] Incorporated by the Glasgow, Barrhead and Neilston Direct Railway Act of 4 August 1845, the line opened in 1848, served by the station known as Barrhead.[100] The striking viaduct built in 1847 at Salterland to carry this line over the Levern survives today (**fig 17**). Built of large rusticated ashlar blocks, it has three arches, the two nearest the west being wide and skewed and the third (east) arch, which crosses over a minor roadway, is a simple round arch with a brick soffit. The company was leased to the Caledonian Railway from 27 September 1849. The line was later extended to Kilmarnock as a joint venture between the Caledonian Railway and the Glasgow and South Western Railway, opening in 1873 as the Glasgow, Barrhead and Kilmarnock Joint Line.[101]

Water supply

The waters of the Levern were managed to suit the needs of the manufactories along its banks, in the form of a succession of weirs or caulds feeding lades parallel to the river. As soon as one spinning mill had utilised its fall the water was extracted for the next one.

Most of the caulds may still be traced and provide the principal archaeological evidence for the industrialisation of the parish. An old weir on the Levern, to the north of Main Street (**figs 10 & 23**), was destroyed only in 1969; some remains of this may be seen above Jubilee Bridge.[102]

The descriptions of the force of the water in the past are hard to match with what remains today: a small watercourse. This famed water-supply, including wells, mill lades, and the river itself, has in part been engineered underground. The wells were all capped off when mains water was introduced in the nineteenth century, this being seen as the only way that sewage management and a safe water supply could co-exist, particularly after cholera epidemics in the 1830s and 1850s.

As the volume of water was small, this meant harnessing all the tributaries in moorland reservoirs, notably the Long Loch, to feed the print and bleach fields and to ensure regularity of supply into the river for the spinning mills. By 1837, a number of reservoirs had appeared, including Harelaw, beyond Fereneze to the north-west of Barrhead. Water for Gateside Bleachworks, later the Barrhead Kid Co, was extracted from Killoch Water above the High Falls.[103]

FIGURE 17
Salterland road and
rail bridges
(*By courtesy of Barrhead and
Neilston Historical Association*)

Place names

By the time of Ainslie's map of the late eighteenth century (**fig 5**), many place names had become more defined or elaborated upon. The locations of Barrhead and Newtown Ralston are indicated – both were evidently places of note by this time. Barrhead itself stretched mostly along the south side of the main Neilston to Glasgow road, while Newtown Ralston (feued from 1780) was located slightly south-west of Barrhead. A cluster of buildings is shown to the west of the road near the Fereneze printfield, and the location of the Levern cotton mill, as well as at least five bleachfields, may be seen. Named buildings were indicated at Rais Tower, Low Arthurley, Mid Arthurley, and Ledronsfield.

The Arthurleys had become Arthurley, and Mid, West, and Low Arthurley, the last the property of Lounds Esq. Aers had become Arrs (now Aurs), Beneth the Kirke was Below the Kirk (modern-day Nether Kirkton), and Chaple was once again in evidence. Ainslie includes Dubs, Fareneze, Lyoncross, Trees, Rawflesh (Rufflees by 1896), Arthiestown, Townhead, Gateside, Waterside, and Dovehill, which are all recognisable as place names today. Broxbar (Bridge Bar), Laigh (Little), and High Auchenbauks (Auchinback) are similarly names that are familiar today.

Population

A census taken in 1811[104] provided the following information about the population, a total of over 2000 persons being distributed thus:

Barrhead village and Newton Ralston (Craigheads)	1230
Grahamston village, including Dealston	448
Gateside and Chappell	394
West Arthurlie	305
Crofthead	394
TOTAL	**2771**

In 1836, it was declared that there were no towns in the parish of Neilston, the populations of the following villages being specified, in families and individuals:[105]

Dovecothall, Barrhead, and Newton Ralston	564	2738
West Arthurlie	79	414
Grahamston	120	595
Gateside and Chappell	140	748
Crofthead, Neilston	118	627
TOTAL	**1021**	**5122**

While it was stated that there was an average of five children in each family, it seems that the average was lowest in the east and north of the area, and highest in the south and west.

In 1837, the greater density of population was noted in the lower (east) part of the parish, which included the Barrhead area. It was also commented upon as to possibly why this area had a higher death rate:

> the greater the poverty of the inhabitants, a greater proportion of them being Irish, and almost exclusively occupied at public works, in trade, or as common labourers. These will perhaps sufficiently account for this striking contrast in the rate of mortality without us to seek for its cause in those differences of climate … It is obvious that the probability of human life here is not great, seeing that two-thirds of the whole population are cut off below 30 years of age. [106]

And when the class of those dying was also taken into account:

> the average ages of … the agricultural population dying in 1825 and 1826 being 60.05; the Scotch manufacturing population being 33.67, whilst the Irish population was so low as 30.19.[107]

Men were old at 45. Manufactures might have been good for entrepreneurs, but living and working conditions came at a harsh price for the workers.

Bleaching and dyeing works

Spinning and weaving technology may have progressed, but cotton and fine-worked muslin goods were still bleached in the local works.[108] The lot of the workers in these industries had improved after agreements were reached between employers and employees in 1853.[109] Before then it was not unknown for the workers to put in sixteen-hour days, and sometimes to continue working all night, to meet the demands of merchants and manufacturers.

In the west of Scotland, a total of 5200 were employed in the bleachworks and dyeworks, of which 4000 were women. Three-quarters of these worked at the drying stoves, where goods were stretched on frames. The thought of between 15 and 40 lightly clad women working together in temperatures between 90° (32°C) and 130°F (54°C) caused a lot of concern amongst many in the community, who were sure that the workers' morals would be in peril.

Specific examples were given regarding the working conditions in the bleach and dye works. Mr J Cochrane Junior & Co of Chapelfield bleachfield[110] reported that of 250 employees, twenty were male and 230 female. They worked for 66 hours a week from 6am until 7pm, and from 6am until 3pm on Saturday, with one and a half hours for meals. Mr James Cunningham & Sons of West Arthurlie[111] employed 260: 60 men and 200 women (more when busy); the youngest employees were aged ten to twelve. The workers worked similar hours to those at Chapelfield, and under similar conditions. The firm was idle for four to five weeks a year, or one day a fortnight, and work slackened off in summer. Cunninghams bleached and finished muslins. Mr Blackwood of Arthurlie, cotton thread and yarn bleacher, employed twenty men and 40 women (when busy, 60). Their working hours were from 6am until 6pm and 6am until 3pm on Saturday.

The bleachfield at Waterside was leased and worked by Andrew Chalmers. It was fed by the largest spring in the parish, Aboun the Brae, that delivered 42 imperial gallons (c 190 litres) per minute.[112] This was also the source for the first waterpipe to the village of Neilston.[113]

Of the works carrying out the Turkey Red dyeing process,[114] it was said that there were six firms in Scotland. Two on the Levern were mentioned in a Parliamentary Paper in 1854/55: Mr Clark's and that of Mr Orr-Ewing on Lower Levern, which was established in 1851.[115] The work was very weather-dependent and so the employees were often idle in winter. In good weather, the 21 processes each took a day to complete, but the process was ongoing: that is, when a piece of cloth had been through process '1', other pieces of cloth were going through processes '2', '3' and so on. For this reason, the hours worked on a Saturday were the same as the rest of the week, 6am until 6pm, with two hours for meals. On Saturdays the women tended to start at 5.30am in order to finish early, often by 3pm or 4pm. The Turkey Red dyers and printworks of Mr Clark Junior on Levern Water,[116] which was established c 1844/45, employed 129 men, of whom 85 were boys under eighteen, and 115 women, 100 and more of whom were under sixteen.

Working conditions in manufacturing textiles in the nineteenth century

The arrival of the power loom in the west of Scotland early in the nineteenth century meant the beginning of a long drawn-out end for the home-based handloom weavers.[117] The poorest of these still operated from home, while others worked in the factory. This continued for 30 years or so. In a similar way to cotton spinning, the mechanisation of weaving meant it could be undertaken by the cheapest labour of all: women and children.[118]

There was government concern about the employment of children in the mills as early as 1816. Of all the manufactories along the Levern, there was just one mill that featured in the 1816 Report of the Select Committee on Children in Manufactories, that at West Arthurlie. Buchanan, Stuart & Lock reported that there were 85 males and 132 females employed; they worked for twelve and a half hours and had one and a half hours for meals per day. Of the total employed, 32 males and 58 females were aged between ten and eighteen years. Of these, six males and six females could not read. There were two males and one female under ten years of age employed; neither male could read.[119] Seventeen years later, another report stated that most mills' hours of employment were twelve to twelve and a half hours, and in 'several districts it was not less than thirteen'. [120] It was 'customary to leave off work on Saturdays in some places one, in others two, hours earlier than on other days. But the time lost on a Saturday is sometimes made up by working a quarter of an hour later on the other days'.[121]

A second round of evidence was collected by the Factory Commission in 1833.[122] The reported conditions at the Broadley [sic] Mill Company in 1833 were probably typical of those experienced throughout the Levern area. There were 248 workers in total. In the spinning department half were male, half female, all operating mules. There were around 60 weavers, all female. Temperatures in the mill were variable; in the web dressing room it was 'not above 75°F [24°C]', and there were five male dressers, four women, and four children working there. The mill had no school and no benefit [Friendly] society, but no corporal punishment was allowed. The workers lived in a nearby village, about five minutes' walk away. Workers' input to the 1833 Factory Inquiry Commission Reports on the Employment of Children in Factories was informative. Alexander Muir (web dresser) thought the temperature was often 80 to 90°F (26–32°C). Catharine Gornly (spinner) worked two wheels containing 232 spindles; she could not write and 'had no learning'. The report concluded that the evidence pointed to 'excessive heat and dust'; with no fanners in the picking room, 'mill cough' was common. The water closets were smelly especially in summer.[123]

A second report of 1833[124] compared the health of children employed in the factories of the Glasgow and Paisley areas for the manufacture of cotton, both weaving and spinning, to that of those still working at home with the poorest handloom weavers. Those children 'who draw over pullies, certain parts of the warp at each traverse of the shuttle in pattern work handloom weaving' are described as 'poor neglected ragged dirty children', who worked thirteen to fourteen hours a day. Aged nine to thirteen, they 'stand on the same spot, always barefooted on an earthen, cold, damp floor all day'.

It was claimed, however (by Bridgeton employers), that the children in the factories were treated with 'almost parental kindness'. The factory-based spinners and power-loom weavers were 'united in close exclusive societies'; there was a 'monopoly of well paid cotton labour', and they were 'able to strike when they please'. Handloom weavers were, by comparison, powerless.

Other comments about the workforce are illuminating: all the adult male spinners chewed tobacco, and none was 'tall and athletic'. Female spinners married young, usually aged seventeen to 22, and some ceased working on marriage; in factories in general, married women were 'living with husbands who are neither employed nor retained but their fertility was not hindered by work'.[125]

Specific reports on the Levern valley mills in 1834 are quite informative: Charles Dunlop's mill (Dovecothall/Levern Mill) was run by water power.

FIGURE 18
Aerial view of Fereneze
Mills, Gateside, undated but
probably 1960s
*(By courtesy of RCAHMS;
© Crown copyright RCAHMS)*

The only part of the mill that was ventilated by fanners (driven off the water wheel) was the picking room; elsewhere doors and windows were simply opened. The youngest employees were aged nine, and mill workers had worked 307 days out of the previous 365. Some 140 of the workers lived in houses owned by their employer; the employer provided free schooling.

The Broadley Mill Company had both cotton spinning and power-loom weaving, both operated by waterpower. The original spinning department was begun in 1791 and weaving began *c* 1828. John Graham's Fereneze cotton spinning mill was erected *c* 1800 (**fig 18**) and was enlarged in 1824. James Orr & Company's Crofthouse [Crofthead] Mill (**fig 19**) prepared and spun cotton; the mill was first erected in 1803, began spinning in 1806, and was extended in 1818.[126] In the 45 years between the compilation of the two *Statistical Accounts,*[127] which provide so much information about this period, John Robertson, foreman at Crofthead, had improved the process of 'backing off'[128] for self-acting mules; the cotton trade was to be grateful – not so perhaps the workforce:

the full-grown operative is dispensed with, and only children required for piecing up the threads, who are now paid one-half more than formerly. ...the mule producing about one-fifth more yarn, whilst the saving upon the wages will be about two-thirds. A third advantage is that it brings the workers under more control of the master.[129]

A further result was that the new unions, or 'combinations', of workers whose power was so loathed by the mill owners, had been dispensed with; 'the service of children only is required'. Like other industries of the period, workers were gradually acquiring rights; until the mill owners defeated the cotton spinners' strike in 1837, mule spinners ran what was virtually a closed shop, and controlled the industry.[130]

Expansion had clearly taken place in the years leading up to 1837: 'Additions have been made to different mills and public works in the parish, some of which have been increased to nearly *double* their original size'.[131] The new parts of these buildings were built of either freestone or whinstone, both of which were available locally.[132] The Dovecothall Mill had acquired a slightly different description from that of 45 years previously:

It is a small building ... containing 3 storeys, 8 feet each in length; is 54 long within, by 24 broad. This mill was the second cotton-mill in Scotland and was built by Stewart, Dunlop & Co. [133]

A further description stated:

according to Mr Wilson[134] [the mill] was 78 feet long and 28 broad. *To this there was added* another mill in 1800, of 123 feet long by 32½ broad, having 5 storeys in it, and to this there was in 1834, added another addition, of 113 feet long by 40 broad – the whole forming an immense pile of building.

An earlier statement in the same description said that the new building was '5 storeys 10 feet high and sunk flat and a garret; and is 113 feet long and 46 feet wide and ... joined to the old mill'.[135]

At South Arthurlie, a new printfield was erected in 1835 for calicoes; it failed in its earliest efforts to produce Turkey Red products even though it employed 500.[136] The site was bought by Zechariah Heys in the 1840s.[137] At the Cross Arthurlie bleachfield, another large print shop was built. [138] At the other end of the river, from Dovecotehall [sic] to Waterside Field, the banks of the Levern were:

thick set with population and public works. ... three large bleachfields, four printfields, a corn and chipping mill, and six large cotton mills, giving employment to a vast number of men, women and children – all active and industrious.[139]

By 1837, the six mills on the Levern had an average production to the value of £139,000;[140] the numbers of men women and children employed in spinning, bleaching and printing were:

	under 12 yrs		under 18 yrs		20 yrs +		TOTAL
	M	F	M	F	M	F	
Cotton-spinners & power-loom weavers	37	39	220	445	296	622	**1659**
Printers etc	290	139	195	122	511	86	**1343**
Bleachers	17	29	49	232	126	259	**712**
Total of each age	344	207	464	799	933	967	**3714**

By the 1860s,[141] west to east, there were the following textile manufactories along the Levern and its tributaries:

Crofthead mill (1792); Broadlie Mill – by then flax (1791); Gatesidemill printworks – silk and cotton (formerly cotton spinning, 1786); Fereneze works (near Gateside converted to cotton in 1801–03), plus bleachworks (further downstream) – the water supply to these at Fereneze had a fall of 35 feet (*c* 10 m);[142] West Arthurlie mill (1795) – cotton, plus West Arthurlie bleachworks and Upper Arthurlie bleachworks, both on the lade off Colinbar Burn; Cross Arthurlie mill – cotton (*c* 1830s muslin weaving factory);[143] Chappell bleachworks (reduced in size, lade gone, and used as Chappellfield laundry by 1896); Fereneze print works (1773, near station); Cross Arthurlie printworks (gone by 1863, replaced by the Arthurlie biscuit factory by 1896); Dovecothall Mill (1780)/Levern Mill (1798) – cotton. In 1857, there was a large reservoir between Cross Arthurlie Road and Bournock [sic] Road (gone by the time of the 1895 Ordnance Survey map).[144] The printworks complex at South Arthurlie (Springfield) lay on another stream to the south.

Wages and hours

The average weekly wages in the manufactories were: [145]

Pattern drawers:	£1 15 shillings
Block-cutters	£1 4 shillings
Printers	£1 1 shilling
Tirers	2 shillings and thru'pence (3d)
Labourers	12 shillings
Women	6 shillings

In the cotton mills, 69 hours were worked per week, and the week was six days. Printers worked from 6am until 6pm in summer, bleachers eleven to twelve hours a day, 72 hours a week. Children aged between eight and fourteen were employed in great numbers; they worked the same hours as men, for between two shillings and sixpence to four shillings a week.[146]

By 1860, men were being inveigled away from the mills into the 'new' heavy industries such as manufacturing and engineering (see below) that were emerging in the area. In a sense this was fortunate, as it was large numbers of women and children, aged over thirteen after the introduction of the Education (Scotland) Act in 1872, that continued to be used as unskilled labour, overseen by men.

Female employment in the cotton industry remained important in Renfrewshire throughout the middle to the end of the nineteenth century. For over 40 years, a quarter to a third of all female employment was in the cotton industry in one way or another.[147] By 1891, cotton's general importance – particularly the weaving and spinning sectors – had dramatically declined but thread retained its dominance in units of great size: two giant firms in Paisley and one in Neilston.

Education in Barrhead

The concerns of the writer of the New Statistical Account becomes apparent when the health and morals of the 'original' inhabitants are contrasted with the 'immoral and irreligious' habits of some of the other residents of the area. It is suggested that the behaviour of those paid 16 shillings to £1 a week was 'frugal, sober and contented', compared with that of those paid £1 10 shillings to £2 10 shillings a week, which was 'dissipated, prodigal, literally wretched and poor'.[148] One group concerned itself with religion, the other with politics: 'they would reform everything, yet refuse to reform themselves'. In addition, the 'baneful' effects of combinations, or unions, and the 'spirit of insubordination and dissatisfaction [seemed] to be spreading amongst the working classes'.[149]

The risk to the morals of the workers, and the effect the lack of education was having on the next generation, led to calls for children to be educated until twelve or fourteen years, and that they not be allowed to work before then. In Neilston parish there were:

> 5 schools attached to 5 of the public works, where the children are taught reading, writing and arithmetic, and there are 4 female schools where the common branches of education, with needle-work, are taught.[150]

Some remains of the old Levern Mill school (built *c* 1805) remained until recently in a wall near St John's church.[151]

Nevertheless, illiteracy continued to be a problem, though the people themselves were well aware of the benefits of education. There were calls for an 'academy' to be located centrally between 'Neilston, Barrhead, Grahamston and Newton Ralston'.[152]

New industries

The parish accommodated a broad range of lesser trades, so as well as the textile workers there were masons, wrights, blacksmiths, stone breakers (for road stone), agricultural workers, and miners for lime and coal.[153] Physical remains of the coalworkings may still be seen. A crownhole exists in the grounds of Wester Hurlet House and further examples may be found opposite Kelburn Street in ground now owned by 'The Volvo'. A lime clamp kiln exists at Townhead.

At the same time that the workforce of the textile industry became more female-dominated, new manufacturing and engineering industries were emerging in the area, many of which needed a male workforce. Skilled workers looked to these new businesses,[154] which included foundries (John Cunningham 1891);[155] rolled iron manufacturers (Lawther & Company 1871);[156] boilerworks (Cochrane's *c* 1864);[157] pirn production (Adair's); and sheet-metal workings (MacCallum's). Perhaps best known of all, the firm of John Shanks of Barrhead dates from 1853.[158] Initially, it produced plumbing materials and brass fittings; the tubal works were in Main Street/Glen Street and later expanded into pottery works at Blackbyres. From 1875 the firm specialised as sanitary engineers, and from the late 1920s the entire business transferred to the site at Blackbyres.

The church

The Reverend Fleming, the local minister (and writer of the 1837 *New Statistical Account*), felt very strongly that his town (although he did not specify whether he was writing about Neilston or Barrhead) should be created a 'burgh of barony, with its magistrates and police, and a good, strong, and efficient jail'. He also called for the Neilston church to be enlarged 'or another built at Barrhead'.[159] While undoubtedly he was pursuing his own agenda, he was clearly also concerned at the evident disharmony between the religions

FIGURE 20
Bourock Parish Church, 2005

FIGURE 21
The former Free Church,
now South Parish Church,
2005 *(Headland Archaeology)*

followed by the manufacturing population in the east of his parish. Fleming's concerns would not have been lessened by the building of St John's Roman Catholic church in Prior Park, on Chapel Brae, in October 1841, which served the needs of both Irish and Highland families – some 2000 individuals.[160]

The Bourock Church of Scotland (**fig 20**) was finally opened in 1840, situated on a little knoll to the north of the Main Street, with Alexander Salmon as its minister.[161] The timing was less than fortuitous, as the Disruption – essentially the rebellion of church ministers against the imposition of heritors' (landowners') decisions on appointees to local churches – took place in 1843. Barrhead was ripe for rebellion against the established order, and the Reverend Salmon supported the division in the church that followed. He and his congregation left the church and it was locked for the following seven years. Their new Free Church of Scotland building, completed in 1846, is situated in the middle of the town, set back a little from the south side of Main Street.[162] The Burgher church, established in 1796, continued and, after the union between it (by then the United Presbyterian Church) and the Free Church in 1900, this building and its congregation became Barrhead Arthurlie United Free Church (now South Parish Church) (**fig 21**).[163]

Dissension was clearly rife in Barrhead, as other 'minority' churches followed, many supported by local manufacturers, some of whom were members of the Free Church and others of the Morrisonian Church in Arthurlie Street, which opened in 1853.[164] Highlanders joined English immigrants from Lancashire in their support of the Methodist Church: early worship taking place in a metal building in Henry Street, and from 1902 in the Methodist stone church in Cross Arthurlie Street, which still exists.[165]

Health and water supply

In November 1843, the Poor Law Inquiry had gathered information from Dr Joseph Bell, surgeon in Barrhead for six years. [166] His role included unpaid visiting of the poor when sick. His comments about the town and its inhabitants are both revealing and horrifying:

> I consider the poor suffer a great deal in consequence of the want of regular medical attendance. Deaths frequently occur without any medical man having seen the deceased person ... called too late ... infectious diseases ... no proper measure taken to prevent the spread of infection ... recovery of patients retarded by want of proper supply of cordials and a nutritious diet ... some benevolent individuals ... In the last three months ... change ... Parish authorities given directions that medical men in cases of destitution accompanied by disease be empowered to give a line to one of the grocers of the town ... by virtue of which to furnish provisions or wine if necessary.

His description of the houses of the poor was equally damning: 'frequently no bedding or bed clothes ... but they were not on the poor roll ... as these were able-bodied poor, including labourers or colliers, who were not eligible for assistance. If the head of the household was ill, they had to 'dispose of every article of furniture to enable him to support his family'.

In the last eighteen months, 'persons in sickness received temporary relief and within the last four months greater liberality was shown towards them. Lately [there was a] great deal of fever ... we have it almost annually – usually through beggars from Glasgow and Paisley'. Because 'some of the houses are too ill ventilated and very damp, so disease spreads'; Bell had seen six individuals in a small bed, 'five with fever'.

The report goes on:

> Many of the houses on the ground floor have beds in a recess with a little straw between them and the earthen floor and the floor is generally damp. I saw two in a bed in a cellar two weeks ago, both with scarlet fever with some gallons of water below the bed. Destitution which I have seen at ordinary times I would attribute chiefly to intemperance through occasional want of employment. [The] insane are provided for by the parish. Insane women live with relatives or are boarded out. The violent

are sent to the lunatic asylum ... Children in the parish are generally vaccinated gratuitously by medical men [but I] have known some fatal cases of smallpox. The last case to appear amongst the poor was in spring 1841. There are no regularly bred midwives in Barrhead. The neighbour women generally officiate. I have known serious consequences arise from the ignorance of these women ...There are certain localities in the town in which disease may be said to prevail ... The people are not cleanly in their habits and the town is imperfectly drained, especially in lower localities... orphan children are well provided for ... In the last two years, temporary aid [has been given] to persons in sickness. We experience great want in our village for not having a place to which persons may be removed who are attacked with fever or other infectious diseases ... the present system of poor law is deficient. [I] consider it a great deficiency in our parish which is a large manufacturing district that no relief is afforded to [the] able bodied when [they are] unable to find employment. The perfect system has a tendency to encourage beggars. Beggars from Barrhead go to Paisley and *vice versa*.

In common with much of Scotland, Barrhead suffered nineteenth-century cholera epidemics. The famed pure water of the area's wells had become contaminated by sewage from the overcrowded town, and the spread of disease followed. The new mains water supply arrived in 1865; a new sewerage system followed soon after, but raw sewage was still discharged into the Levern.[167] Yet Barrhead was to make a leading contribution to sanitary engineering across the UK through the well-known firm John Shanks of Barrhead.

Moves towards burgh status

In 1837 both Barrhead and Neilston were still villages, although it was conceded that both were 'moving towards [town] status'.[168] There was no recognisable infrastructure in place:

neither magistrate, nor police, nor jail ... kept in order by active Justices of the Peace, with a constabulary at their command. ... a small debt court held in Neilston and Barrhead alternately, once a month, by the Justices. On these occasions, they have their legal assessor and clerk. ... the nearest market town is Paisley, but there is no occasion to go thither ... Every article and convenience of life is to be had in the parish.[169]

The parish was 'inhabited chiefly by the proprietors or owners of large manufactories, their foremen and operatives'.[170] In 1818, the Justices of the Peace included the industrialists Henry Dunlop (Arthurlie), Gavin Ralston (Ralston), and Alexander Graham (Fereneze). William Lowndes of Nether Arthurlie represented slightly 'older' money in the area.[171] From 1812 cotton mills were not an outlet for the small-scale investor, but was rather business on a vast scale, with 'an average of 13,000 spindles ... installed in each of the six Neilston mills'.[172] Barrhead was beginning to flourish: little wonder that there were calls for its status to be recognised and for it to be upgraded to burgh status.

In 1836, a branch of the Glasgow Union Bank was established in Neilston; the Levern Mechanics' Institution (1825)[173] had a library of note;[174] and there were seven Friendly Societies in the parish. Those quick to claim assistance from the parish poor roll were the English and the Irish, not locals.[175] In 1837, Barrhead also had a post office [176] The town held just one fair a year, for horse-racing, and a cattle-market was held on the last Friday and Saturday of June.[177] With 58 inns and alehouses in the parish as a whole, it is a fair assumption that Barrhead, with half the parish population, perhaps had half of them.[178]

Barrhead had evidently become a dynamic town; no wonder the 'parent' parish of Neilston in the form of the Reverend Fleming regarded the lower Levern area with horror. Not only was it full of dissenters, incomers, and independent thinkers, but the many female workers wore very little at work (because of the heat) and the male workers had plenty of money to spend on drink.

Barrhead might not have been a burgh, but its Gas Light Company, located near Glen Street, dated from 1833[179] and a police force was established by 1857.[180] In 1861, the Young Men's Mutual Improvement Association, a Free Church organisation, was formed.[181] Barrhead people were organised enough to register their own Co-operative Society in 1861, one of the earliest in Scotland.[182] By 1887, there were 1600 members and the main shop was at Bourock, Main Street. Branches were located at Dovecothall, Grahamston, and Main Street, Neilston, and departments included grocery, drapery, boots and shoes, tailoring, coal, and baking.[183] The plan of the bakery is extant in the Dean of Guild papers.[184] The occupations of the fourteen founder members gives a good indication of the make-up of pre-burgh Barrhead: brass founder, pattern maker, millwright, furnaceman, iron moulder (three), engineer, bleacher, calico printer, iron turner, iron dresser, mechanic, and cotton carder.[185]

By the time Wilson's *Gazetteer*[186] appeared in 1882, under the entry for Neilston parish, Barrhead was described as a 'town', West Arthurlee, Newton Ralston and Gateside as 'villages', and Cross Arthurlee and Grahamston as 'suburbs'.

The Burgh

Many industrial towns achieved independence after 1862, under the terms of the General Police and Improvement (Scotland) Act of that year which allowed towns with a population of over 700 to become 'Police Burghs'. This gave the right to levy rates for such issues as lighting, paving, cleaning streets, improvement of water and gas supplies, prevention of infectious diseases, regulation of slaughter houses, and control of vagrants.

The Burgh of Barrhead[187] finally came into being when, in December 1893, the Sheriff Court of Renfrew and Bute at Paisley determined that, based on the number of 'dwelling-houses therein and the density of the population [Barrhead] is in substance a town and is suitable for being formed into a police burgh', under the Burgh Police (Scotland) Act 1892. Gateside was excluded 'at the wish of the mill owners within it' (**figs 22 & 23**). [188] The issue of Barrhead's status had been raised almost half a century before, but had failed to make any progress. In the *Paisley Journal* of 7 January 1854, it was stated that 'nothing has ever been found in Paisley Sheriff Court Records to indicate that boundaries were ever fixed'.[189]

Barrhead's elevation to burgh status coincided with the economic changes of the 1890s.[190] With William Shanks as Barrhead's first provost (1894–96) it is perhaps not surprising that early burgh records are full of references to ashboxes and ashpits, and to sewage processing.[191] The health of the burgh's residents was closely linked to the state of the water supply and sewage disposal. The water supply was to be improved, and Manchester's experience of the International System, the 'most approved and satisfactory', was salutary.[192] The Co-operative Society gifted two drinking fountains, one at Carlibar Road, 'opposite the entrance to the railway station', and another 'at the foot of Craigheads Street in Main Street'.[193] Dean of Guild plans of 1894–96 show the site of the new purification works.[194]

Despite the introduction of mains water from 1865, Barrhead residents were still 'drinking their drains' as foul water contaminated ground water, wells included. It was acknowledged that even though a proper drainage scheme was started in 1896, it was likely that for 'some time – with opening up old closed drains and other filthy places, there may be an increase in the infectious cases'.[195]

Each month between May and September 1896, between 50 and 111 ashpits and 456 to 656 ashboxes were cleaned, and in November applications were made for an extension to the main sewer. A visit was made to Exeter to examine the sewage disposal system there. The new bacterial sewage works opened in June 1899.[196] By November 1899, the numbers of bins, pits, and boxes that had to be dealt with each month had substantially increased: 3292 ashbins, 62 ashpits, 36 cartloads of manure, and 238 cartloads of rubbish were recorded. Not surprisingly, the council agreed to supply the staff with jackets, leggings and sou'westers – at 8s 4d each.[197] Extant Dean of Guild plans of 1894–96 show the design of a 'dung pit' in Henry Street.[198]

The provision of urinals was also a matter for the council: one (with two compartments) at the railway station, and singles at Cross Arthurlie Street and adjoining the gasworks were to 'be filled up with enamelled backs and flushing

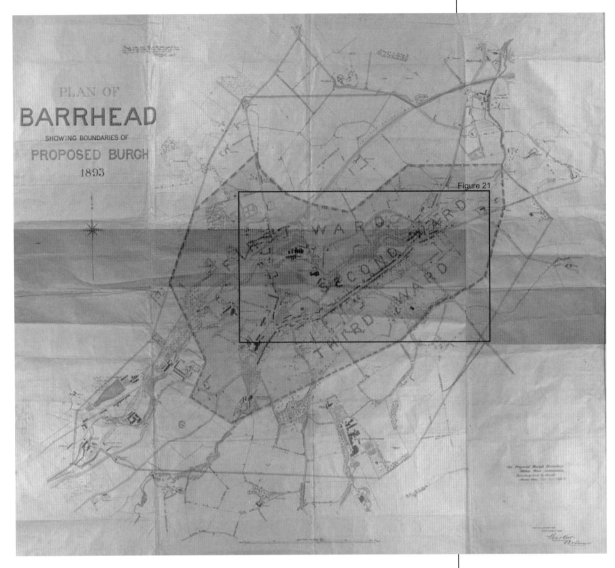

PLAN OF
BARRHEAD
SHOWING BOUNDARIES OF
PROPOSED BURGH
1893

Figure 21

tanks'.[199] The Dean of Guild plans indicate the growing interest in improving hygiene. Wash houses were proposed for Victoria Place, at the Co-op in Main Street, and at Mary Street, amongst others in the period from 1894 to 1896; and laundries were to be set up at Henry Street for a Mr Wilson and in John Street for Bailie Cochrane.[200] Plans of the proposed and existing sewers in Water Road, Bowershall, Carlibar Road, Hillside Road, Glasgow Road, Cloth Street, and Neilston Road, amongst others, are still extant and give clear indication of the improvements taking place at the end of the century.[201]

In spite of these improvements, disease was still causing concern to the Medical Officer. The year 1895 'has not been a very healthy one for the burgh' it was reported,[202] with 165 deaths, giving a mortality rate of 19.22 per 1000, in a population of 8280 people. Forty-eight children did not survive to one year, and there were four deaths of people of over 80 years.

There were 298 births, and of these 13 or 14 per cent were illegitimate. There were also 42 cases of infectious diseases, and twenty of these were located in the Cross Arthurlie and Grahamston districts; the other 22 were spread over Kelburn Street, Main Street, Craigheads, Dunterlie, and Dovecothall. The diseases were:

14	scarlet fever
14	typhoid fever
9	erysipelas
3	diptheria
2	puerperal fever

The following year was not much better: diphtheria, scarlet, typhoid, and enteric fever were rife in November and December 1896, and houses and apartments were disinfected as a result. Seven dairies, three milk shops,[203] and two slaughterhouses were visited and found to be clean; common lodging houses too were visited and checked. As well as lodging houses, ordinary dwellings came under examination, and the 1895 ruling on chimney size was perhaps the first of many measures introduced.[204]

One of the earliest desires of the council was that it should obtain control of the roads within the burgh,[205] and within two years parts of Barrhead were being improved. The private streets of Robertson Street, Cogan Street, and Water Road gave concern in 1896, particularly relative to drainage. Temporary repairs were to be made 'until connections with the main drain were effected'; costings were made for causewaying Cross Arthurlie Street 'as compared with cost [of] macadamising the same'.[206] Two years later, repairs were in hand at Robertson Street (from 16 March until 11 April 1898) following subsidence,[207] and the macadamising of nearby Cogan Street 'unless the necessary consents were obtained at once [to] call upon the owners to causeway the street'.[208] The specifications, estimate, and tender for the upgrading of Cogan Street are extant and detail precisely how the routeway was to be excavated, what use might be made of the existing material, the whinstone kerbstones sizes, the dressing of the causeway in the water channels, the bottoming, metalling, and rolling of the surface, and the formation of footpaths. Should the contractor damage any gas or water plugs or manholes he was to replace these at his own expense.[209]

Just sixteen years after the burgh was created, it was noted that 'the streets have undergone great improvement at the hands of the Council'[210]. The Carlibar bridge at Dovecothall was rebuilt and widened in 1901. The pavements were made of ash, with that from the station to Cross Arthurlie causing some concern,[211] although in 1897, the council was beginning to ask that the 'footpavements' be paved with 'Granolithic or Caithness [stone] from Darroch's property to Fereneze back gate in Carlibar Road ... also ... opposite Gilliesdam in Cross Arthurlie Street ... [where] Caithness [stone was to be used]'.[212] Evidently there was a desire to see new building work in the burgh conform to the Dean of Guild's regulations.[213] Streets were lit between May and the autumn holiday,[214] and the number of streets lit was extended to Cogan Street, Barnes Street, and Henry Street 'adjoining Mr Cowan's stables'.[215] A new fire station was in place by 14 December 1896.[216]

The burgh officials were keen to show that Barrhead was at last a bona fide burgh. From 1899, the council leased for three years Elgin Villa, Lowndes Street.[217] New municipal buildings were proposed in 1900, designed by Ninian McWhannell and John Rogerson,[218] and completed in 1904 (**fig 24**). Both are built of bull-faced red sandstone with polished ashlar dressings. Their style is described as 'Free Scots Renaissance', separated by a lane entered through a pair of 'wrought-iron gates with thistle and lion rampant motifs'.[219]

Railways

Barrhead's close relationship with the railways increased further once it became a burgh; a number of lines crossed the town, serving the many industrial sites (**fig 25**). There were as many as five separate railway stations,[220] including Barrhead New, which was never opened, and Barrhead Central, which opened in October 1902 and closed

FIGURE 24
Burgh Chambers, Main Street, 2005

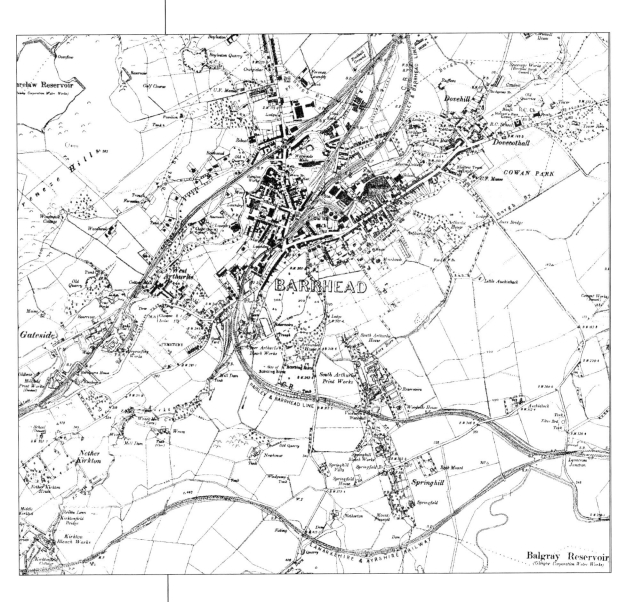

at the beginning of 1917; it was never again used.[221] The only surviving line today is that of 1848, the earliest built (see above), which became part of the London, Midland & Scottish Railway in 1923.

On 14 December 1896, the Burgh Council[222] was discussing a proposal for a Paisley and Barrhead District Railway.[223] A new railway station would be required, and also bridges over Cross Arthurlie and Kelburn Street.[224] In 1899, the discussions had moved on to concerns about the bridge being erected by the Paisley and Barrhead District Railway Company over Kelburn Street; the bridge position was evidently encroaching on to the street line by at least 12 feet (c 3.5 m). The upshot was that the railway company was to pay for the improvements of the street at Cross Arthurlie Corner, and 'the throwing back of the Hall at the Constitutional Club'. By the end of 1899, the council

FIGURE 26
Paisley and Barrhead District
Railway Company viaduct
(By courtesy of Barrhead and
Neilston Historical Association)

FIGURE 27
Remnants of the viaduct
in 2005

was applying to the Court for compulsory acquisition of the club ground.[225] Eventually a splendid viaduct (parts of which remain today beside a Tesco supermarket; the rest is demolished) carried the line over these streets, and through Springhill on a viaduct (**figs 26 & 27**). One description compared the viaduct favourably to that at Berwick-upon-Tweed; it had 38 arches and was built of white freestone.[226] Cochrane Street appeared as a result of the new line, and Central Station was located there.[227] In 1902, the company became part of the Caledonian Railway (which already ran the 1848 line) and the whole complex formed part of the London, Midland & Scottish Railway from 1923.[228]

Housing expansion

New buildings of this period included the Co-operative building in Graham Street (**fig 28**), and those on the east side of Cochrane Street by builders Houston & Young, who also constructed most of Glen Street.[229] Many tenements were built in late nineteenth-century Cogan Street, Gertrude

Street, Paisley Road, and Gladstone Avenue, for example, and the extant Dean of Guild plans show that the whole town was expanding.[230] A typical plan of two tenements at Graham Street indicates that they were to house four families, each flat having one large living area, called 'kitchen', and two bedrooms. The four flats shared a communal wash house, with washing tub and a wc. This small outside building was to have a concrete roof with a pipe for ventilation and an ash bin.[231] Tenements in Cross Arthurlie Street have been modernised in recent times by Barrhead Housing Association.[232]

The twentieth century

Employment

By the beginning of the twentieth century, calico printing was in decline across Scotland. In 1899, the Calico Printers' Association was formed, probably in response to the general decline in the industry, with fourteen firms of printers from Scotland and 32 from England. Together they produced dress goods, furnishings, linings, flannelettes, and mixed fabrics. They included the Millfield Printworks in Gateside, which shut c 1901. After 1918, there was a further decline in the cotton industry and several smaller Scottish firms closed down.[233] A new factory was established in Barrhead in 1919, however, a Hat and Cap Factory known as 'The Globe' on Paisley Road.[234] With the decline of the textile industry, many of the rows of single-storey houses that made up the original mill villages were also deemed beyond saving.

In the twentieth century, Barrhead was home to an array of industries. Amongst these were Yorkshire Imperial Metals, who came to the burgh in 1938, making copper tube at a site on Paisley Road,[235] and Shanks, who by 1959 employed 1600. Other industries in Barrhead in 1961 employed chiefly skilled manual labourers. They included glass and ceramics production; furnace, forge, foundry and rolling mills; engineering and allied trades; textile works (mostly female workers); transport and communications; warehousing; clerical (male and female); sales (male and female); service, sport and research (more female than male); and professional and technical, again employing more females than males. [236]

The firm of Scottish Animal Products, which produced canning equipment, came to Barrhead in 1964, later becoming Spillers Ltd. In 1968, advertisers in the Barrhead official guide included Scottish Wool Bleachers and Dyers Ltd at Arthurlie Works; Hugh Alexander and Sons Ltd, Waterside Mills, Cross Arthurlie Street – yarn spinners to the carpet and knitwear trade; and Scottish Fellmongers Ltd at West Arthurlie Skin Works, which dealt with 'all classes of domestic pulled wool'.[237]

With changes in the British economy, Barrhead's industrial base has altered; sites once wholly given over to the textile industry have been reused, often a number of times, and many are now clear of industrial activity.

Transport

Trams linked Barrhead to Paisley by 1907, to Neilston *c* 1910, and to Glasgow by 1912.[238] Plans in the Dean of Guild papers indicate the layout of the tramways and associated buildings.[239] A number of roads were widened to accommodate the tramlines and properties disappeared; one loss was Allan's shop, which was next to the Arthurlie Inn, now remembered in the name of the new roundabout close by.[240] By 1959, however, a 'tramway abandonment project' was underway to remove the redundant tramlines from the roads.[241] From the 1930s, buses too offered transport to and from Barrhead.[242]

New entertainments and housing

The Dean of Guild papers monitor closely the expansion of the burgh.[243] By 1908 the town would have the amenity of a skating rink in Barnes Street. This must have proved popular as it was extended in 1910.[244] The Dean of Guild papers contain a plan, in the same year, of a drill hall, including a miniature cartridge range.[245] By 1922 the town could boast a picture house in Cross Arthurlie, with 618 seats in the stalls and a further 234 in the balcony.[246]

The Masonic Temple (Category C(S)-listed) in Cochrane Street was built in 1910 to a design by Ninian McWhannell and John Rogerson, it is constructed of Giffnock stone and is in the Scots Baronial Revival style (**fig 29**).[247]

FIGURE 29
Masonic Temple, Cochrane
Street, 1975/76
*(By courtesy of RCAHMS;
© Crown copyright RCAHMS)*

In 1919, the council bought land along Arthurlie Street and built 110 houses there; soon Kerr and Blackwood Streets followed.[248] This enabled slum clearance to begin and so came the end of the old 'raws': Printers' Raw, Monkey Raw, Ragman Raw, and Glow'rin Raw. The Salt Lake area was also demolished. Dovecothall, Graham Street, and Main Street, particularly *nos* 194 to 318, were to be redeveloped. The part of Glen Street that runs up to join Main Street was a new addition to the burgh in the 1920s/1930s,[249] and the Bowershalls scheme was completed in 1925. This was built 'to suit a different class of tenant and naturally these were let at a cheaper rent of £1 and 8 shillings, but it was found that the same old problems of overcrowding returned'.[250] The new housing areas of Springhill and Dovecothall sprang up in the interwar period (**fig 34**). Electricity replaced gas in the burgh during the 1920s.[251]

The Second World War would have an impact on Barrhead's townscape. Once the Co-operative Society had cleared away its blitz-damaged (13 May 1941) properties on Main Street, it was decided that a new street line was to be adopted. The new frontages were built out of alignment with the older buildings, as may be seen to this day.[252] After the Second World War, the housing situation was so bad that new estates were built, located at Trees, Crossmill, Dunterlie, Arthurlie, and Auchenback.[253] Housing was also needed to accommodate the overspill of Glasgow people who moved to Barrhead.[254] The expansion of the town continued, further suburbs being created in the 1960s, and the housing at Auchenback being extended *c* 1968.[255]

Postscript

Barrhead was to change radically in the twentieth century. The historic core now reveals little of its industrial past, but public buildings remind the passer-by of the importance to Barrhead of its burgh status (**fig 24**). Tower Rais (now Montford House, Darnley Road) and its associated buildings echo the fine buildings of the later nineteenth century, old mansions still stand but with new uses, and new buildings and road alignments reflect the change of priorities in a more modern age. The boundaries of the burgh were extended in the 1920s, and again in 1947, and by 1972, Barrhead covered 1200 acres (c 485 ha). A population of 6069 in 1851 had risen to 18,289 by 1971. The small, dirty textile settlements on the banks of the Water of Levern have become the modern, clean town of Barrhead with its beautiful riverside walks.

Notes

1   J McWhirter, *Mine Ain Grey Toon, the story of Barrhead from prehistoric times to 1914*, proved particularly relevant.

2   A MacQuarrie, 'The historical context of the Govan stones', in A Ritchie (ed), *Govan and Its Early Medieval Sculpture* (Stroud, 1994), 27–32

3   *Ibid*

4   J R Allen and J Anderson, *The Early Christian Monuments of Scotland: a classified illustrated descriptive list of the monuments with an analysis of their symbolism and ornamentation* (Edinburgh, 1903), 454

5   D Craig, 'The early medieval sculpture of the Glasgow area', in Ritchie, *Govan and its Early Medieval Sculpture*, 73–87

6   R N Bailey, 'Govan and Irish Sea sculpture', in Ritchie, *Govan and its Early Medieval Sculpture*, 113–19

7   Craig, 'The early medieval sculpture of the Glasgow area', in Ritchie, *Govan and its Early Medieval Sculpture*, 73–87

8   *OSA*, xiii, 148

9   NAS, RHP 12652, 'Plan of the estate of Hawkhead, revised from the OS' (1885)

10   McWhirter, *Mine Ain Grey Toon*, 6

11   Kirkconnel Parish Heritage Society website, www.kirkconnel.org

12   *Ibid*

13   So noted in the Chartulary of the Abbey of Paisley according to *NSA*, vii, 307–08

14   McWhirter, *Mine Ain Grey Toon*, 10, 17

15   I B Cowan and D E Easson, *Medieval Religious Houses in Scotland* (London, 1976), 173

16   McWhirter, *Mine Ain Grey Toon*, 15

17   *Ibid*, 16

18   So noted in the Chartulary of the Abbey of Paisley according to *NSA*, vii, 307–08

19   *NSA*, vii, 322

20   *Ibid*, 323

21   McWhirter, *Mine Ain Grey Toon*, 14

22   M Donnelly, 'Levern Walkway, Barrhead, East Renfrewshire' (GUARD unpublished archive report, 1999), 5; McWhirter, *Mine Ain Grey Toon*, 14

23   Donnelly, 'Levern Walkway', 5

24   *Ibid*, 14–15

25   I Hughson, *Bygone Barrhead* (Ochiltree, 1993), 12

26   McWhirter, *Mine Ain Grey Toon* , 15

27   *RCHAMS Record no NS55NW 1*

28   McWhirter, *Mine Ain Grey Toon*, 11–12

29   *Ibid*, 14

30   *Ibid,* 40

31   M Hughson, 'Grain Mills in Neilston Parish' in *Renfrewshire Local History Forum J*, vol 6 (1994) 14–19

32   McWhirter, *Mine Ain Grey Toon*, 20

33   *Ibid*, 23

34   *Ibid*, 31; taken from the poll tax roll of 1695, which would be a good starting point for further research into the distribution of occupations by settlements.

35   W Roy, *Military Survey of Scotland* (1747–55) Available: www.scran.ac.uk. The area covered inconveniently straddles a join in the maps.

36   McWhirter, *Mine Ain Grey Toon*, 33, 43; in 1857 this was called Cotton Street.

37   D Pryde, *A History of the Parish of Neilston* (Paisley, 1910), 84, dates Newton Ralston as *c* 1773; McWhirter, *Mine Ain Grey Toon*, 30. Newtown Ralston later became Craigheads, possibly named for the Craig family that took over the Cogan mills at Cross Arthurlie *c* 1843.

38   Pryde, *History*, 84

39   McWhirter, *Mine Ain Grey Toon*, 33–4

40   *Ibid*, 34. We are indebted to Mrs Maud Devine for her assistance.

41   *Ibid*, 24–5

42   The Secession church later united as the United Presbyterian Relief Church (the Arthurlie United Free Church) *NAS*, CH3/342

43   McWhirter, *Mine Ain Grey Toon*, 24, 48. This building was demolished in 1968.

44   *OSA*, xiii, 150. McWhirter, *Mine Ain Grey Toon*, 31, states that in 1755 the population was *c* 600 in the Barrhead area, rising to 1000+ by 1798.

45   McWhirter, *Mine Ain Grey Toon*, 33

46   McWhirter, *Mine Ain Grey Toon*, 33, is particularly detailed on this.

47   Pryde, *History*, 84–5

48   McWhirter, *Mine Ain Grey Toon*, 27–8

49   Children's Employment (Mines) Commission, *Parliamentary Paper*, 1842, vols XVI–XVII, 350

50   Information from Historic Scotland Statutory List.

51   *OSA*, xiii, 155

52   A Slaven, *The Development of the West of Scotland: 1750–1960* (London, 1975), 97–9

53   *OSA*, xiii, 155

54   Slaven, *Development*, 88

55   Place name spellings used here are those from the OS map of 1896.

56   *OSA*, xiii, 165; working conditions on the bleachfields led the workers astray: 'the work people upon them are exposed much to wetness and cold... [which] is apt to lead to the too frequent use of spiritous liquors...'.

57   *Ibid*, 145

58   *Ibid*, 146

59   *NSA*, vii, 335

60   McWhirter, *Mine Ain Grey Toon*, 38; steam-powered copper rollers were introduced here in 1831.

61   W Roy, *Military Survey of Scotland*, 1747–55

62   Flax-weaving process producing plaited bands and also clothing trims, shoelaces, ties, belts, musket braids, hat bands, leg ties, girdles; also referred to as ribbon weaving.

63   *NSA*, vii, 335

64   J R Hume, *The Industrial Archaeology of Scotland, I: Lowlands and Borders*

(London, 1976), 216–17

65 McWhirter, *Mine Ain Grey Toon,* 35; he states that the second bleachfield was at Low Arthurlie. The date of 1765 is confirmed by Children's Employment (Mines) Commission, *Parliamentary Paper,* 1842 vols XVI–XVII, 350.

66 McWhirter, *Mine Ain Grey Toon,* 29. Children's Employment (Mines) Commission, *Parliamentary Paper* 1842, vols XVI–XVII, 350 states that the first printfield was established in 1770, and the first cotton mill in 1780.

67 S M Nisbet, The Rise of the Cotton Factory in Eighteenth Century Renfrewshire (PhD thesis Paisley University 2003)

68 Slaven, *Development,* 92–5

69 *OSA,* xiii, 149

70 *NSA,* vii, 336 gives the date 1778 but the site was not rented until 1779. Nisbet (*Renfrewshire Local History Forum J* vol 2, 1990) established that spinning started in June 1780.

71 *OSA,* xiii, 153; Factory Inquiry Commission Reports, *Parliamentary Paper,* 1834, vol XIX Part II, Report *no* 133 reports that the mill built by Charles Dunlop was erected in 1792. This report appears to relate to the two mills of Dovecothall Mill, hence two starting dates of 1780 and 1792.

72 Hume, *Industrial Archaeology,* 217. The mill depicted in fig 4 is in fact Fereneze Mill. The Gateside mill further upstream has below-ground archaeological potential, as well as a high dam and an outflow to the other side of a small bridge.

73 *OSA,* xiii, 153

74 *Ibid*

75 *Ibid,* 154

76 *Ibid,* 216–17

77 *NSA,* vii, 336. Some have argued that the correct date is 1803.

78 Slaven, *Development,* 85

79 McWhirter, *Mine Ain Grey Toon,* 38; the site of the present sewage works.

80 We are indebted to Mark Watson for this information. The Factory Commission returns PP 1834 XIX 190–1 were provided to him by John Shaw, in which it is stated that the first part of the mill was built for flax-spinning in 1798, and after a fire in 1801 was converted to cotton spinning.

81 W W Knox, *Hanging by a Thread: the Scottish cotton industry, c 1850–1914* (Preston, 1995) 42

82 McWhirter, *Mine Ain Grey Toon,* 38; they worked at the calico Corse Mill *c* 1770 onwards.

83 *Ibid,* 43; demolished to make way for new houses at Sproull Place.

84 I Hughson, *Barrhead and Neilston in Old Picture Postcards* (Zaltbommel/ Netherlands, 1985; 3rd edn, 1993), pl 20

85 McWhirter, *Mine Ain Grey Toon,* 43

86 *OSA,* xiii, 149

87 McWhirter, *Mine Ain Grey Toon,* 41

88 *Ibid,* 34

89 *Ibid,* 35

90 *Ibid,* 33

91   *OSA*, xiii, 153

92   McWhirter, *Mine Ain Grey Toon*, 48

93   *OSA*, xiii, 164

94   *Ibid*

95   Children's Employment (Mines) Commission, *Parliamentary Paper*, 1842, vols XVI–XVII, 350

96   McWhirter, *Mine Ain Grey Toon*, 27

97   *NSA*, vii, 340

98   www.neilston.org.uk/history/villagedevelopment.htm.

99   *NSA*, vii, 351

100   Hughson, *Barrhead and Neilston*, pl 26

101   NAS, British Railways Board records: BR/GBN, 1856–57; J Thomas, *A Regional History of the Railways of Great Britain 6: The Lowlands and the Borders* (revised edn, Newton Abbott, 1984), 125–6. From 1923, the Caledonian Railway became part of the London, Midland & Scottish Railway.

102   McWhirter, *Mine Ain Grey Toon*, 35. We are indebted to Mrs Maud Devine and Mrs Irene Hughson for their assistance.

103   Information from Stuart Nisbet, who has surveyed the water system.

104   Quote comes from McWhirter, *Mine Ain Grey Toon*, 31; possibly the census discussed in Children's Employment (Mines) Commission, *Parliamentary Paper*, 1842, vols XVI–XVII, 350, although this information is not confirmed.

105   *NSA*, vii, 330

106   *Ibid*, 314–15, 338

107   *Ibid*

108   Bleaching Works, *Parliamentary Paper*, 1854–58, vol XVIII

109   *Ibid*, 62

110   *Ibid*, xxvi

111   *Ibid*, 62

112   *NSA*, vii, 315

113   We are indebted to Mrs Irene Hughson for her assistance.

114   Process by which cotton cloth was dyed with scarlet pigment obtained from the root of the madder plant (see article by L Arthur at www.scottishtextiles.org.uk; 'process was a foul, costly complex method').

115   Bleaching Works, *Parliamentary Paper*, 1854–58, vol XVIII, xxxiv

116   *Ibid*, 67

117   The Poor Law Inquiry (Scotland), *Parliamentary Paper*, 1844, vol XXV, 149 stated that the handloom weavers were the lowest class in Neilston parish, earning five shillings a week.

118   Slaven, *Development*, 104

119   Report of Select Committee on Children in Manufactories, *Parliamentary Paper*, 1816, vol III; Abstract of the Returns made by the Proprietors and Managers of Cotton Mills in Scotland, 240.

120   Factory Inquiry Commission Reports, *Parliamentary Paper*, 1833, vol XX; First Report of the Central Board of HM Commissioners – the Employment of Children in Factories. Northern District: reports of examinations taken before Mr Stuart, 7.

121 *Ibid*

122 Factory Inquiry Part II Supplementary Report, *Parliamentary Paper*, 1834, vol XX, 190*ff*; gives an explanation of terminology and work in cotton manufacturing in Britain.

123 *Ibid*, 115

124 Factory Inquiry Commission Reports, *Parliamentary Paper*, 1833, vol XXI; Factories. Second Report of the Central Board of HM Commissioners for Inquiring into the Employment of Children in Factories – Medical Report by Sir David Barry. Report on Bridgeton handloom weavers, regarding their employment throughout the Glasgow and Paisley areas, 4.

125 *Ibid*, 72–3

126 Factory Inquiry Commission Reports, *Parliamentary Paper*, 1834, vol XIX, Part II, 188, 190–1, 194

127 The two accounts are: J Monteath, 'The Parish of Neilston' (1792) in *OSA*, and A Fleming, 'The Parish of Neilston' (1837) in *NSA*.

128 *NSA*, vii, 327, does not specify exactly what this was. It was a step in the shift from manual to water-powered equipment that meant that less strength was necessary to operate the machinery. Knox, *Hanging by a Thread*, 48–9, states that the first self-acting machine was invented by Richard Roberts of Manchester, in 1825.

129 *NSA*, vii, 327. The author praised this move, while seemingly ignoring the impact of this development on his later calls for the same child workers to be educated.

130 Knox, *Hanging by a Thread*, 145–64

131 *NSA*, vii, 329, 336

132 *Ibid*, 329

133 *NSA*, vii, 336; Slaven, *Development*, 93, holds that it was the third after Penicuik 1778 and Rothesay 1779.

134 *NSA*, vii, 336 No indication is given as to who Mr Wilson was; the dimensions given are the same as those given by Monteath in 1792.

135 *NSA*, vii, 329

136 *NSA*, vii, 317; C Taylor, *The Levern Delineated in a Series of Views of the Most Interesting Scenery along the Banks & Vicinity: with historical and topographical sketches* (Glasgow, 1831), 9, suggests it was a bleachfield, then a Turkey Red dyeworks.

137 McWhirter, *Mine Ain Grey Toon*, 38; Bleaching Works, *Parliamentary Paper*, 1854–58, vol XVIII, 67 – Mr Heys is not mentioned; Heys' closed in 1930, having been one of the most important industries of Barrhead.

138 *NSA*, vii, 329

139 *Ibid*, 317

140 *Ibid*, 336–7

141 Ordnance Survey map of Barrhead & Neilston, 1863/64. Available: www.old-maps.co.uk

142 Taylor, *Levern*, 8

143 McWhirter, *Mine Ain Grey Toon*, 37

144 'Renfrewshire', Ordnance Survey, 2nd edn, 1:2500 scale (sheet XII.15, 1896)

145   *NSA*, vii, 337

146   The Poor Law Inquiry (Scotland), *Parliamentary Paper*, 1844, vol XXV, 149

147   *Ibid*, 25

148   *NSA*, vii, 332

149   *Ibid*, 338

150   *Ibid*, 346–7

151   McWhirter, *Mine Ain Grey Toon*, 37. We are indebted to Mrs Maud Devine for her assistance.

152   *NSA*, vii, 346–7; confirmed by The Poor Law Inquiry (Scotland), *Parliamentary Paper*, 1844, vol XXV

153   The Poor Law Inquiry (Scotland), *Parliamentary Paper*, 1844, vol XXV, 149

154   Pryde, *History*, 85, lists an enormous number of different industries.

155   NAS, CS 318/34/69, John Cunningham engineer, iron founder, 1891

156   NAS, CS 318/14/211, Lawther & Company, rolled iron manufacturers, 1871

157   Glasgow University Archives: GB0248 GD 329/10, Records of John Cochrane & Co (Barrhead) Ltd, boilermakers and pump manufacturers, East Renfrewshire, 1897–1950

158   NAS, CS 318/21/448, 1878; CS 318/31/298, 1888, John Shanks, brass founder sanitary engineer; Glasgow City Archives, TD7 10, Catalogue of Shanks & Co, 1906

159   *Ibid*, 351

160   McWhirter, *Mine Ain Grey Toon*, 41, 52. In August 1941, St John's burned down; a new church opened at Dovecothall in 1962.

161   NAS, Church of Scotland records: Barrhead Chapel, 1859–1949

162   NAS, Church records, CH3/870, 1850–1934. It became Barrhead South (United Free and later Church of Scotland) and since 1985 has been joined with Levern and Nitshill as Barrhead South & Levern.

163   NAS, Church records, CH3/342, 1796–1951. Following a further union between it and the Church of Scotland in 1929 it became the Barrhead Arthurlie Church of Scotland; two years later it united with Barrhead Westbourne as Barrhead Arthurlie.

164   McWhirter, *Mine Ain Grey Toon*, 50. In later years this was the EU Congregational Church.

165   McWhirter, *Mine Ain Grey Toon*, 53; NAS, Church records, CH11/57/8, nd: papers relating to the history of Methodism in Barrhead (and other places). Access restricted.

166   The Poor Law Inquiry (Scotland), *Parliamentary Paper*, 1844, vol XXII, 419–20

167   McWhirter, *Mine Ain Grey Toon*, 46

168   *NSA*, vii, 339

169   *Ibid*, 339; McWhirter, *Mine Ain Grey Toon*, 32; the JP court met the first Monday in every month, sometimes at Cowan's Hotel, Foundry Brae.

170   *NSA*, vii, 329

171   McWhirter, *Mine Ain Grey Toon*, 32

172   Slaven, *Development*, 97

173   McWhirter, *Mine Ain Grey Toon*, 56

174   *NSA*, vii, 348

175   *Ibid,* 349

176   *Ibid,* 340

177   *Ibid,* 349; McWhirter, *Mine Ain Grey Toon,* 67; the horse race ceased in 1863.

178   *NSA*, vii, 349

179   *Ibid*, 56; NAS, Gas Board records, GB1/7/1–6, 1868–1949; Hard coal for gas was obtained from Muirkirk, 30 miles away, *NSA*, vii, 349

180   McWhirter, *Mine Ain Grey Toon,* 90

181   McWhirter, *Mine Ain Grey Toon,* 76; later YMCA

182   Hughson, *Bygone Barrhead*, 2; McWhirter, *Mine Ain Grey Toon,* 51; founder members were supporters of the Morrisonian Church.

183   *Co-operative Directory*, 1887

184   Plans passed by the Dean of Guild, *no* 51 1900, 1902–03

185   R Murray, *History of the Barrhead Co-operative Society Limited* (Barrhead Co-operative Society Ltd, 1911), 4

186   J Wilson, *The Gazetteer of Scotland* (Edinburgh, 1882)

187   McWhirter, *Mine Ain Grey Toon,* 79–81 provides details of the first Town Council election results.

188   Barrhead Burgh Records, Minute Book i, (1896), 1, 2, 14–15

189   Quoted in R M Urquhart, *The Burghs of Scotland and the Police of Towns Act 1850* (Motherwell, 1989), 51, footnote 16

190   Hughson, *Barrhead and Neilston in Old Picture Postcards*, introduction

191   Barrhead Burgh Records, Minute Book ii, (1896), 20, 43, 81, 12

192   Barrhead Burgh Records, Minute Book ii, (1896), 3

193   *Ibid,* 131–2

194   Dean of Guild Plans for Burgh of Barrhead, 1894–96, *no* 35

195   *Ibid*, ii, 385

196   Pryde, *History*, 89

197   Barrhead Burgh Records, Minute Book iii, (1898/99), 25 September 1899–27 December 1899, 4 December 1899

198   Dean of Guild Plans for Burgh of Barrhead, 1894–96, *no* 18

199   Barrhead Burgh Records, Minute Book ii, (1896), 132

200   Dean of Guild Plans for Burgh of Barrhead, 1894–96, *nos* 13, 25, 33, 21 and 38

201   Dean of Guild Plans for Burgh of Barrhead, 1897–98, *no* 8; Dean of Guild Plans, 1898, *nos* 19, 20, 22, 24, 25, 26 and 30

202   Barrhead Burgh Records, Minute Book i, (1896), 384, 385

203   With cow-sheds, conditions in dairies and milk shops were regulated even before the burgh came into being; Barrhead Burgh Records, Minute Book i, (1896), 339, 341

204   *Ibid,* 391

205   *Ibid,* 49

206   Barrhead Burgh Records, Minute Book ii, (1896), 131

207   *Ibid*, 403

208   *Ibid*, 388

209   Dean of Guild Plans, 1898, *no* 43

210   Pryde, *History*, 85

211 Barrhead Burgh Records, Minute Book ii, (1896), 95

212 *Ibid,* 122, 163

213 Barrhead Burgh Records, Minute Book iii, (1898/99), 25 September 1899–27 December 1899, 12 September 1898

214 Barrhead Burgh Records, Minute Book ii, (1896), 120

215 *Ibid,* 122

216 *Ibid,* 134

217 Barrhead Burgh Records, Minute Book iii, (1898/99), 25 September 1899–27 December 1899, 20 March 1899, 8 May 1899 Described first as Elgin Villa, then Elgin Cottage.

218 Hughson, *Bygone Barrhead,* 3

219 Both are listed Category B; information from the statutory list notes.

220 Hughson, *Bygone Barrhead,* 32

221 RCAHMS: photograph and text RE/1544

222 Barrhead Burgh Records, Minute Book ii, (1896), 133

223 NAS, British Railways Board Records: BR/PBD, 1896–1902; include minutes and reports

224 Hughson, *Barrhead and Neilston,* pl 27

225 Barrhead Burgh Records, Minute Book iii, (1898/99), 25 September 1899–27 December 1899

226 Pryde, *History,* 88

227 Hughson, *Bygone Barrhead,* 32

228 NAS, British Railways Board Records: BR/PBD, 1896–1902; notes

229 McWhirter, *Mine Ain Grey Toon,* 44

230 Dean of Guild Plans for Burgh of Barrhead, 1899, eg *nos* 13 and 27

231 Dean of Guild Plans for Burgh of Barrhead, 1897–98, *no* 8

232 Hughson, *Bygone Barrhead,* 44

233 *Ibid,* 7; McWhirter, *Mine Ain Grey Toon,* 39

234 Dean of Guild Plans for Burgh of Barrhead, 1914–22, *no* 44

235 *Burgh of Barrhead – Official Guide* (np, 1968)

236 *Census of Scotland 1961*: Occupation and Industry; County Tables, Renfrew

237 *Burgh of Barrhead – Official Guide*

238 Pryde, *History,* 88

239 Dean of Guild Plans for Burgh of Barrhead, 1910–13, *nos* 5, 6, 7, 8, 9, 10 and 12

240 Hughson, *Barrhead and Neilston,* pl 24, 25

241 D MacLachlan, 'The Burgh of Barrhead', in the 'County of Renfrew and Bute' – *The Third Statistical Account of Scotland* (Glasgow, 1962), 278

242 Hughson, *Bygone Barrhead,* 35

243 Dean of Guild Plans for Burgh of Barrhead, 1902–03, *nos* 3 and 6; 1904–05, *nos* 2, 3 and 29; 1906–09, eg *no* 34

244 Dean of Guild Plans for Burgh of Barrhead, 1906–08, *no* 41; 1910–13, *no* 15

245 Dean of Guild Plans for Burgh of Barrhead, 1910–13, *no* 13

246 Dean of Guild Plans for Burgh of Barrhead, 1914–22, *no* 19

247 Category C(S)-listed; information from the statutory list notes.

248 Barrhead Reminiscence Group, *Barrhead & Levern – Then and Now* (Strathclyde Regional Council, nd), 37

249 Hughson, *Barrhead and Neilston,* pl 32, 33

250 Barrhead Reminiscence Group, *Barrhead & Levern – Then and Now,* 37

251 MacLachlan, 'The Burgh of Barrhead', 278

252 *Ibid, 279*

253 *Ibid*

254 Barrhead Reminiscence Group, *Barrhead & Levern – Then and Now,* 37

255 *Burgh of Barrhead – Official Guide*

4 The potential of Barrhead

(See **fig 35**)

Medieval and earlier remains

There is a possibility that remains of prehistoric settlements survive somewhere beneath the modern town, particularly close to old watercourses, but the town's extensive modern development has reduced the potential for these remains to survive. More likely is the possibility that an early ecclesiastical site may lie unrecorded beneath the south-west part of the town. The presence of the Arthurlie cross-shaft and the map evidence attesting to another cross stone, now lost, suggests that the area has the potential to contain such a site. The obvious location for any early church is associated with the holy well dedicated to St Connel and the medieval Chapel of Ferm (**fig 34**), but equal consideration should be given to the corresponding southern side of the valley, where both crosses appear to have been located.

Barrhead came into existence only in the later eighteenth century. Before this time the area was farmed and interspersed with scattered small settlements. Several of these were associated with the lands of Arthurlie, but there are also examples at Aurs, Auchenback, and Dovecothall. It is not known when these were created but they seem likely to have their roots in the medieval period. The locations of most now lie beneath housing estates constructed in the last century, although some traces may survive below ground.

It is easier to pinpoint a location for both the Chapel of Ferm and Stewart's Rais (**fig 34**). Excavations have established that the lowest courses of stonework associated with the Rais survive, and there is a high potential for ancillary buildings to survive in the surrounding area. There seems a good chance that remains associated with the chapel survive on the level terrace around the current Chappell House.

The road running through the town, now known as Main Street, was in use by the medieval period and probably earlier. In addition, there seems to have been a bridge, or perhaps a ford, over the Levern Water at Bridgebar (**fig 6**) since the later sixteenth century or earlier, and archaeological remains relating to a medieval predecessor may survive below ground.

To the north of the bridge, Pont's map indicates that there was a tower at this location in the late sixteenth century (**fig 6**), although the building is not marked on Ainslie's plan of 1796 (**fig 5**). Given the inaccuracy inherent in these early maps it is not possible to determine the exact location of this tower but it may well have been on the north-east fringes of the town.

FIGURE 30
Nineteenth- and early twentieth-century buildings, south side of Main Street, 2005

FIGURE 31
Buildings at rear of Main Street, 2005
(Headland Archaeology)

63

Post-medieval town and mills

Considerable redevelopment has occurred along Main Street, which developed from the late eighteenth century as the town's textile industry boomed. The extent of both the town and the surrounding industries by the end of the nineteenth century is shown on **fig 35**. A group of early buildings survives on the south side of Main Street (**fig 30**). The buildings preserved within this group vary from small weavers' cottages likely to date to the early nineteenth century to early twentieth-century public buildings celebrating the town's elevation to burgh status. Several small, presumably late eighteenth- or early nineteenth-century industrial buildings survive to the rear of the Main Street properties (**fig 31**).

The prospects for archaeological deposits surviving beneath these buildings are higher than beneath more modern developments and the structures themselves may well contain elements of earlier buildings. The archaeological potential of this group should be viewed as additionally important because of its rarity.

The mills that were pivotal to the town's development no longer survive as standing structures. Some upstanding foundations relating to the West Arthurlie Mills (where there is also an ancillary building (**fig 32**)), and to

FIGURE 32
Ancillary building at West
Arthurlie Mill

a lesser extent Levern Mills do survive. The former is likely to include the archaeology of terraced cottages and the mill school. The latter are presented to the public in a park setting. Gateside Mill has been undisturbed since demolition. Here, and on the other sites, some remains are likely to survive below the surface as archaeological features (**fig 33**).

In particular, it may be assumed that wheel pits, which are lined in ashlar and below floor level, have a high chance of survival.[1] Their location can often be pinpointed through the use of Ordnance Survey plans. Many mills, including Fereneze, will have had an eighteenth-century timber wheel, followed later by a detached wheelhouse with a larger, iron wheel.

Even where no upstanding remains are apparent, foundations may survive and can provide valuable information. Regular ashlar blocks that supported drives to the paired drum frame on the upper floors were found this year at Cromford Mill, Derbyshire, and should the opportunity arise these should be looked for at the sites of Dovecothall/Levern, Broadlie, Crofthead, Cross Arthurlie, Fereneze, and Gateside mills.

Summary of archaeological potential of mill sites in Barrhead

Name	Founded and early owners	Function and occupier, 1856 OS Namebook	Later function	20th-century status	Archaeological potential
Dovecothall or Levern Mill	1778 Ramsay, Leviston and Love. Later Stewart Dunlop and Co	Cotton spinning and weaving, own gaslight; Dunlop and Son	A park	Dem	High
West Arthurlie Mill	1791 Stewart Dunlop and Co	Cotton mill; Mitchell and Lock (with school and 3 rows of cottages)	Light engineering	Dem	High
Cross Arthurlie Mill	1825 Martin & Lee, fine net weaving, bankrupt 1826	Cotton spinning and weaving; John and Robert Cogan (restarted 1837)	Imperial Laundry	Dem 1982	Low
Fereneze Works	1798 Bailie Cochrane, flax 1801 Mr Graham, cotton	Cotton spinning mill and bleachworks; James and William Wallace	Clyde Waterproofing Company	Dem 1990	Low
Gateside Mill	1786 James Dunlop	Gateside Mill Print Works in 1856. Own gaslight. McFarlane Ligat and Craig	Millfield Printworks closed 1901	Dem	High
Broadlie Mill	1791 Mr Airston 1828 Pollock Gilmour & Co 1834 Broadley Mill Co 1850 Rattray and Thomson	Flax spinning and weaving by water and steam. M C Thomson	After 1872 used for cloth finishing. Now Clyde Leather Co	Standing	High
Crofthead Mill/ Crofthouse Mill	1792 Stewart, Orr and Co, second mill 1818	Cotton Mill; The late Mr Orr	English Sewing Cottons Ltd	Standing Listed category B	High

Several water-powered mills used gas for lighting. Excavations at Stanley Mills, Perthshire, revealed some enigmatic vaults that might have been involved in this process, but further examples need to be recorded in order to allow interpretation. The water seals for the iron gas-holders were achieved by means of an ashlar lining in which the iron plates would sit. A section of river embankment recently fell into the Cart at Busby revealing an iron gas-holder, and it is apparent that evidence may survive below ground around the mills.[2]

Very importantly, evidence of the gathering and use of water by the mills can be revealing. It should be assumed that there is the potential to recover valuable archaeological information concerning these processes along all river banks and the courses of lades and ponds. Structures such as sluices and weirs may survive on the Levern Water, where at least one example of the former can still be seen (**figs 13 & 34**). The site of Fereneze Mills (**figs 15 & 18**), just outside the town, has been recently redeveloped for housing; a culvert arch which survives on the fringes formerly carried a railway line over a lade within the mills.

Investigation before any redevelopment could reveal valuable details about the industries on which the town depended and grew. Given that very deeply cut features, such as wheel pits, may have survived even extensive redevelopment, these sites should be investigated where the opportunity arises.

Many of the large post-medieval villas set within their own parkland around the town survive, such as Arthurlie House (**fig 16**) and Fereneze Golf Clubhouse (formerly Trees). Not only will archaeological preservation be better in their surrounding undeveloped grounds but, as reflected in their designation as Category B-listed buildings, the houses and gardens are themselves of interest.

Further work

At first glance Barrhead does not appear to have a rich archaeological heritage but research for this Survey suggests there is still much to surprise beneath what appears to be a very modern town. Only systematic archaeological survey in likely locations can further our knowledge of the area's history before the town emerged. Archaeology and building recording also have a role to play in filling gaps in the historical documentation for later periods, especially in recovering information about the ordinary townsfolk who helped create the town by their labours in the mills and bleachfields.

Bleachworks and printworks used copious quantities of water, and because of resulting contaminants at these sites, and at gas works, it is possible that the Council will have commissioned a contaminated land survey which includes historical research. It was not possible in the time available for this Survey to pursue this potential source of useful information.

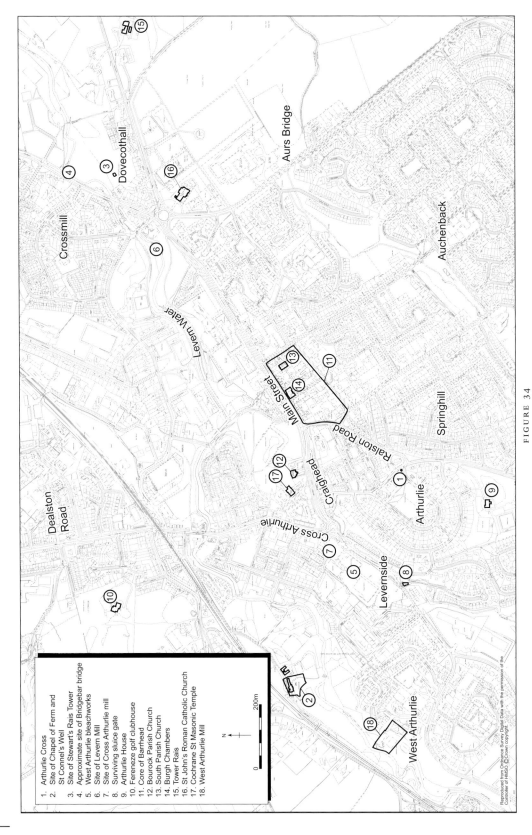

1. Arthurlie Cross
2. Site of Chapel of Ferm and St Connel's Well
3. Site of Stewart's Rais Tower
4. Approximate site of Bridgebar bridge
5. West Arthurlie bleachworks
6. Site of Levern Mill
7. Site of Cross Arthurlie mill
8. Surviving sluice gate
9. Arthurlie House
10. Fereneze golf clubhouse
11. Core of Barrhead
12. Bourock Parish Church
13. South Parish Church
14. Burgh Chambers
15. Tower Rais
16. St John's Roman Catholic Church
17. Cochrane St Masonic Temple
18. West Arthurlie Mill

Crossmill

Dovecothall

Aurs Bridge

Auchenback

Levern Water

Main Street

Raiston Road

Craighead

Cross Arthurlie

Arthurlie

Springhill

Levernside

Dealston Road

West Arthurlie

N

0   200m

Reproduced from Ordnance Survey Digital Data with the permission of the
Controller of HMSO. ©Crown copyright.

FIGURE 34

Areas and locations mentioned in *Historic Barrhead* (*Prepared by Headland Archaeology; based on OS mapping;*
© Crown copyright All rights reserved. Historic Scotland Licence no. 100017509 [2008]))

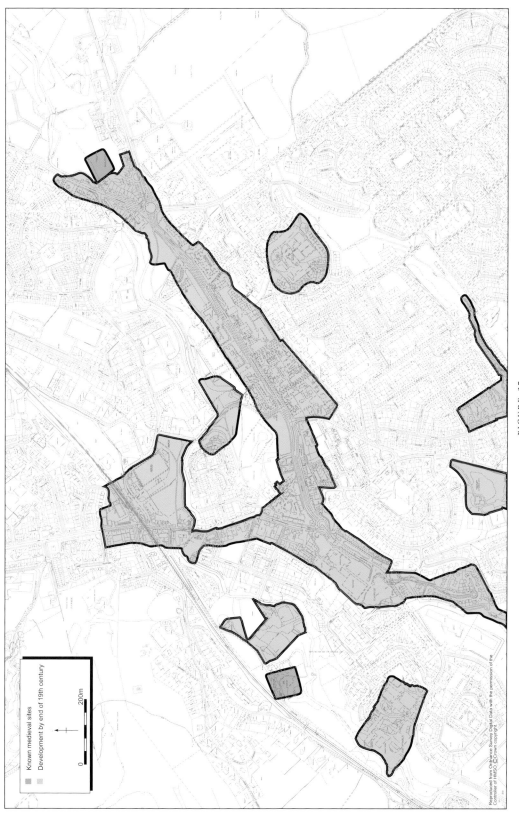

Known medieval sites

Development by end of 19th century

0   200m

FIGURE 35

Plan showing areas that had been built up by *c* 1900. See also the broadsheet map for water-powered sites along the Levern Water. Where development is being
considered, whether or not shown on this map, archaeological advice should be sought from the Local Authority

(Prepared by Headland Archaeology; based on OS mapping; © Crown copyright All rights reserved. Historic Scotland Licence no. 100017509 [2008]))

A more detailed survey of the surviving early buildings in the town could also be carried out. This could record the distribution of surviving weavers' cottages for example, both from cartographic sources and by field examination of upstanding structures.

There are a number of documentary sources that were not assessed for this Survey which would in all probability give a greater depth of understanding of Barrhead, in particular the changing townscape of the twentieth century. The first three Council Minute Books (1896–99) were trawled, but time did not allow a study of the later volumes held at the East Renfrewshire Library at Giffnock. There are further Barrhead records, dating from 1931 to 1960, deposited in Glasgow University Archives (GB 0248 TSB 071); these were not assessed. The Dean of Guild Records, mainly plans, are an excellent source of information on the built environment (now deposited at Whitehaugh Barracks, Paisley). Any further research into the townscape of Barrhead should consider in greater depth these important records.

The ledgers of Barrhead industrialists have been used in this Survey, but further research might pay dividends. Much of the Shanks documentation has seemingly disappeared, but there are a few documents still extant which have not been assessed. There are, for example, in the Court of Session papers deposited in the National Archives of Scotland, some pertinent to John Shanks, brass founder and sanitary engineer, dated 1878 (CS 318/21/448) and 1888 (CS 318/31/298). There is also a catalogue of Shanks & Co (TD7 10), dating to 1906, in Glasgow City Archives.

The Court of Session papers also include papers pertinent to John Cunningham, engineer and iron founder, dated 1891 (CS 318/34/69), and to Lawther & Company, rolled iron manufacturers dating to 1871 (CS 318/14/211). The records of John Cochrane & Company (Barrhead) Ltd, boilermakers and pump manufacturers, dating from 1897 to 1950 are held in the Glasgow University Archives (GB 0248 GD 329/10). All of these would give a further insight into the industries and working conditions of Barrhead in the nineteenth century, as might the Gas Board records from 1868 to 1949 (NAS, GB1/7/1–6).

The Scottish Co-operative Wholesale Society had a strong presence in Barrhead. Their records from 1826 to 1980 are deposited in Glasgow City Archives. These include those of Bainsford and Grahamston Baking Co-operative Society from 1867 to 1919, of Barrhead Co-operative Society from 1860 to 1980, and of Grahamston and Bainsford Co-operative Society Ltd, from 1870 to 1881. All of these would merit attention and might give a further understanding of the town. The British Railways Board records from 1856 to 1857 (NAS, BR/GBN) and from 1896 to 1902 (NAS, BR/PBD) include minutes and reports that might offer further information on the important transport connections to Barrhead.

A fuller understanding of the social life in Barrhead might be gained from church records. In the National Archives of Scotland, the Church of Scotland records include those for Barrhead Chapel dating from 1859 to 1949 (CH2/1421). Deposited also are church records from 1913 to 1931 (CH3/1457) and those of Barrhead, Westbourne United Free Church Kirk Session, Church of Scotland. There are also papers relating to the history of Methodism in Barrhead (CH11/57/8). School records, such as those of Grahamston Public School, dating from 1887 to 1944 (GCA, CO2/5/6/4), and the logbooks of Barrhead Public School from 1873 to 1928 (GCA, CO2/5/6/6), would be of great interest. These are deposited in Glasgow City Archives. Also in this repository are the records of Paisley Savings Bank. It is possible that these too might throw further light on life in Barrhead.

General surveys for the nineteenth century, such as *Fowler's Directory* of Renfrewshire, which dates from 1832 to 1834, and the County Survey and the *Third Statistical Account,* for the twentieth century, would also give a broad overview of the changing townscape. The poetry and stories of the calico workers would also merit examination, as would an assessment of local matters in the *Barrhead News*. The work of Dennis Topen in the Braes Country Park and the volume *Prehistoric Renfrewshire Papers in Honour of Frank Newall*, edited by D Alexander, would give telling insights into earlier ages.

Although a small town, with an ever-changing character, it is very clear that there is a great wealth of documentary material, particularly for the twentieth century, awaiting further study; this will give an even fuller understanding of the built environment and townscape of Barrhead.

Notes

1   Mark Watson provided helpful comment concerning the archaeological potential of these sites

2   Watson pers comm, following its discovery at Busby by Stuart Nisbet

Glossary of technical terms

Anglo-Saxons	People who settled in Britain from the Low Countries and Germany in the fifth or sixth centuries AD; also described as Angles and Anglian.
bleachfield	Grassed areas where lengths of cloth (linen and cotton) were laid out to bleach in the sun; continuous watering was needed. Dutch and Irish techniques were more advanced and workers were brought to Scotland to teach the necessary skills. Later, sheds were used, and a mix of ashes and sour milk was poured onto the cloth. This was a lengthy process taking four to five months, as each time the cloth was washed and exposed to sunlight. New techniques *c* 1749 reduced this to four to five days: sulphuric acid replaced the milk. In 1799, a dry bleaching powder was introduced to Scotland via Charles Macintosh and Charles Tennant. The latter, working a bleachfield in Waulkmill Glen, Barrhead, later founded the St Rollox chemical company, Glasgow.
Bronze Age	Prehistoric period between the Neolithic and the Iron Age *c* 2000– 500 BC in Scotland.
Burghers	With Anti-Burghers as their opposition, a split of the Secession Church over the issue of the taking of a Burgess Oath (an anti-Catholic move of 1745).
CANMORE	A computerised database maintained by RCAHMS which covers the whole of Scotland and contains information on many standing buildings, chance finds, and archaeological sites.
cholera	Infectious bacterial disease of the small intestine, causing vomiting and diarrhoea.
Covenanters	Followers of radical Calvinist type of Presbyterianism *c* 1638 and after.
Crompton's mule	Spinning machine that combined the roller drafting of Arkwright's water frame with the action of Hargreaves' spinning jenny. Initially hand-powered, at least in part, and particularly suited to spinning of weft yarns, the machine became the mainstay of the British cotton and woollen industries through much of the nineteenth century.
diphtheria/croup	Infectious bacterial disease of the throat.
enteric fever	*see* typhoid

erysipelas	A streptococcal infection, inflaming the skin, especially on the face.
inkle	Flax-weaving process producing plaited bands and also clothing trims, shoelaces, ties, belts, musket braids, hat bands, leg ties, girdles; also referred to as ribbon weaving.
Iron Age	The final prehistoric period, running in Scotland from *c* 500 BC to AD 400, although the latter half is often termed the Roman Iron Age.
lint	flax
Neolithic	Meaning 'New Stone Age' and in Scotland representing the period of human settlement between *c* 4000 – 2000 BC.
Picts	The peoples occupying northern Scotland, as described by the Romans and Anglo-Saxons.
piecers	Spinning workers, usually little girls, who repaired broken threads.
pirn	A reel, bobbin or spool onto which wool, cotton etc is wound.
post-medieval	The period from the sixteenth to the eighteenth century.
power loom	A weaving loom worked by mechanical power.
printfield	In 1742 calico printing was introduced to the west of Scotland, Dutch and English printers being encouraged to come and teach their skills. In 1771, the Crum family opened the Levern printfield, followed by Fereneze (1773) and Thornliebank (1779). From the 1780s on, bleachers were also dyers and printers. From 1785 cylinder printing replaced block printing. The debris and dyes from printfields was emptied into the streams, contaminating them and killing all the fish.
puerperal fever	Fever following childbirth caused by uterine infection.
scavengers	Spinning workers, usually female, who removed the cotton waste from the machines.
secession	Act of withdrawing from membership of a body, in this case from the Church of Scotland.
toll	A charge made to pass a particular point on a road, usually to assist with maintaining the road.
Turkey Red dyeing	Process by which cotton cloth was dyed with scarlet pigment obtained from the root of the madder plant (see article by L Arthur at www.scottishtextiles.org.uk; 'process was a foul, costly complex method').
turnpike road	A road on which a toll is collected.

typhoid/enteric fever	A disease caused by Salmonella typhosa which enters the body through contaminated food or water and passes into the bloodstream, causing blood poisoning. After seven days, spots appear, followed after ten to fourteen days by fever and diarrhoea/constipation; can cause heart failure. Cause discovered 1880–84.
typhus	A disease spread via lice, the cause of which was discovered in 1916. A victim scratches a bite and rubs infected lice faeces into the wound. It is controlled by washing / improved hygiene.

Bibliography

Manuscript sources and maps

British Library, London (BL)

Map C9b4	W Roy, *Military Survey of Scotland*, 1747–55
	Available: www.scran.ac.uk

East Renfrewshire Library, Giffnock

Barrhead Burgh Records, Minute Books, 1896–99

Glasgow City Archives

CO2/5/6/4	Grahamston Public School, 1887–1944
CO2/5/6/6	Barrhead Public School, logbooks, 1873–1928
CWS	Scottish Co-operative Wholesale Society, 1826–1980, including:
	Bainsford & Grahamston Baking Co-operative Society, 1867–1919
	Barrhead Co-operative Society, 1860–1980
	Grahamston & Bainsford Co-operative Society Ltd, 1870–81
TD7 10	Catalogue of Shanks & Co, 1906
TD1212	Calico Printers' Association; plan of Gateside mill

Glasgow University Archives

GB 0248 GD 329/10	Records of John Cochrane & Co (Barrhead) Ltd, boilermakers and pump manufacturers, East Renfrewshire, 1897–1950
GB 0248 TSB 071	Records of Paisley Savings Bank, Barrhead branch, 1931–60

National Archives of Scotland (NAS)

British Railways Board records

BR/GBN	1856–57
BR/PBD	1896–1902

Church of Scotland records

CH2/1421	Barrhead Chapel, 1859–1949

Church records

CH3/342	Barrhead (Burgher) Associate Session, United Presbyterian, Arthurlie United Free and Church of Scotland, 1796–1967
CH3/1457	Barrhead, Westbourne United Free Church Kirk Session, Church of Scotland, 1913–31

CH11/57/8   papers relating to the history of Methodism in Barrhead
     (and other places), nd. Access restricted.

Court of Session papers

CS 318/34/69   John Cunningham, engineer, iron founder, 1891
CS 318/14/211   Lawther & Company, rolled iron manufacturers, 1871
CS 318/21/448   John Shanks, brass founder, sanitary engineer, 1878
CS 318/31/298   John Shanks, brass founder, sanitary engineer, 1888

Gas Board records   GB1/7/1–6, 1868–1949

RHP 6677   Plan of Fereneze Estate, the property of Alexander
                   Graham, 1811
RHP 6679   Gateside, lands of, feuing plan, the property of Alexander
                   Graham of Capeller, 1853
RHP 6680   Gateside Print Works, the property of Messrs Hall and
                   Craig, 1874
RHP12652   Plan of the estate of Hawkhead, revised from the OS, 1885
RHP 45963   R Kerr, Plan of Barrhead showing boundaries of proposed
                   burgh, 1893
RHP 32867   *Plan showing the proposed new boundaries of the burgh of
                   Barrhead, Paisley, 5 December 1929*

National Library of Scotland, Edinburgh (NLS)

Adv MS 70.2.9   T Pont, 'Renfrewshire', *c* 1560–1614 (Pont 33)
Adv MS 70.2.10   R Gordon, 'Barony of Renfrew', *c* 1636–52 (Gordon 55)
WD3B/27   J Blaeu, 'The Baronie of Renfrow', 1654
EMS.b.2.1 (15)   H Moll, 'The Shire of Renfrew with Cuningham', 1745
Newman 645   J Ainslie, 'Map of the County of Renfrew', surveyed 1796,
                   published 1800
Newman 732   J Ainslie, 'Map of the southern part of Scotland', 1821
EMS.s.712 (12)   J Thomson, 'Renfrew Shire', 1826

Whitehaugh Barracks, Paisley

Dean of Guild Plans for Burgh of Barrhead, 1894–1922

Primary printed sources

Census of Scotland 1961: Occupation and Industry; County Tables, Renfrew
Census of Scotland 1971: 1, pt 5; County Reports (Renfrew)
Co-operative Directory 1887: information provided by Gillian Lonergan, Archivist,
     The Co-operative College, Manchester. Available: www.co-op.ac.uk
Crawfurd, G, *The History of the Shire of Renfrew* (Paisley, 1782)
Fowler's Directory of Renfrewshire, 1832/34
Ordnance Gazetteer of Scotland: A Survey of Scottish Topography, F H Groome (ed)
     (Edinburgh, 1883)

The New Statistical Account of Scotland (1837), 307–52 Available: www.edina.ac.uk

The Statistical Account of Scotland 1791–99, Sir John Sinclair (ed), New edition I R Grant and D J Withrington (eds) (Wakefield, 1978), 141–65 Available: www.edina.ac.uk

Wilson, J, *The Gazetteer of Scotland* (Edinburgh, 1882)

Parliamentary Papers

Bleaching Works, vol XVIII, 1854–58

Children's Employment (Mines) Commission, vols XVI–XVII, 1842

Factory Inquiry Commission Reports, vol XX; First Report of the Central Board of HM Commissioners – the Employment of Children in Factories. Northern District: reports of examinations taken before Mr Stuart, 1833

Factory Inquiry Commission Reports, vol XXI; Factories, Second Report of the Central Board of HM Commissioners for Inquiring into the Employment of Children in Factories – Medical Report by Sir David Barry, 1833

Factory Inquiry Part II Supplementary Report, vol XX, 1834

Factory Inquiry Commission Reports, vol XIX Part II, 1834 [includes reports relating to mills belonging to C Dunlop, Neilston (erected 1792); the Broadley Mill Company, Neilston (erected 1791); J Graham, Neilston (erected 1800, enlarged 1824); J Orr & Company, Neilston (erected 1803, enlarged 1818)]

Report of Select Committee on Children in Manufactories, vol III; Abstract of the Returns made by the Proprietors and Managers of Cotton Mills in Scotland, 1816

The Poor Law Inquiry (Scotland), vols XXII, XXV, 1844

Printed books, articles and theses

Alexander, D (ed), *Prehistoric Renfrewshire Papers in Honour of Frank Newall* (Renfrewshire Local History Forum, 1996)

Allen, J R and Anderson, J, *The Early Christian Monuments of Scotland* (Forfar, 1903)

Bailey, R N, 'Govan and Irish Sea sculpture', in A Ritchie (ed), *Govan and its early Medieval Sculpture* (Stroud, 1994), 113–19

Barrhead and Neilston Historical Association, *Local Heroes: the stories of some of the people from the Neilston and Barrhead area who have left their mark on history* (Glasgow, 1986)

Barrhead (Renfrewshire) The Official Guide (Cheltenham, 1938)

Barrhead Reminiscence Group, *Barrhead & Levern – Then and Now* (Strathclyde Regional Council, nd)

Blackburn, M and Clark, S, 'Cross Arthurlie Mill', in *Scottish Industrial History,* **5** (1982), 56–62

Burgess, M, *Discover Barrhead and Neilston* (Renfrew District Council, 1992)

Burgh of Barrhead – Official Guide (1968)

Butt, J, 'The Scottish Cotton Industry during the Industrial Revolution, 1780–1840', in L M Cullen and T C Smout (eds), *Comparative Aspects of Scottish and Irish Economic and Social History, 1600–1900* (Edinburgh, 1977), 116–28

Catling, H, *The Spinning Mule* (Lancashire Library, 1986)

Cooke, T E, 'Notice of a cross-shaft at Arthurlee, Renfrewshire', *Proc Soc Antiq Scot*, **9** (1870–72), 451–2

Cowan, I B and Easson, D E, *Medieval Religious Houses in Scotland* (London, 1976)

Craig, D, 'The early medieval sculpture of the Glasgow area', in Ritchie 1994, 73–87

Cramp, R, 'The Govan recumbent cross-slabs', in Ritchie 1994, 55–60

Darton, M, *The Dictionary of Place Names in Scotland* (Orpington, 1994)

Darvill, T, *Prehistoric Britain* (London, 1987)

Donnelly, M, 'Levern Walkway, Barrhead, East Renfrewshire' (Unpublished GUARD client report, 1999)

Durie, A J, *The Scottish Linen Industry in the Eighteenth Century* (Edinburgh, 1979)

Ferguson, M, *How we came by Barrhead (the first hundred years of town and community* (Barrhead, 1998)

Gifford, J and Walker, J A (eds), *The Buildings of Scotland: Stirling and Central Scotland* (London, 2002)

Hanson, W S, *Agricola and the Conquest of the North* (London, 1987)

Hughson, I, *Barrhead and Neilston in Old Picture Postcards* (Zaltbommel/Netherlands, 1985, 3rd edn, 1993)

Hughson, I, *Bygone Barrhead* (Ochiltree, 1993)

Hughson, I, *Gateside in the nineteenth century* (Barrhead and Neilston Historical Association Occasional Paper, nd)

Hume, J R, *Industrial Archaeology of Scotland I: The Lowlands and Borders* (London, 1976)

Institute of Geological Sciences, *The Limestones of Scotland* (Edinburgh, 1976), 160

Keay, J and Keay, J (eds), *Collins Encyclopaedia of Scotland* (London, 1994)

Knox, W W, *Hanging by a Thread: the Scottish Cotton Industry, c 1850–1914* (Preston, 1995)

Laing, L R, *The Archaeology of late Celtic Britain and Ireland c 400–1200 AD* (London, 1975)

MacLachlan, D, 'The Burgh of Barrhead', in the County of Renfrew (eds: Moisley, H A and Thain, A G) and the County of Bute (eds: Somerville, A C and Stevenson, W) – *The Third Statistical Account of Scotland* (Glasgow, 1962), pp 275–87

Macquarrie, A, 'The historical context of the Govan stones', in Ritchie 1994, 27–32

McWhirter, J, *Mine Ain Grey Toon; the story of Barrhead from prehistoric times to 1914* (Barrhead, 1970)

McWhirter, J, *Barrhead Co-operative Society 1937–1961* (Barrhead Co-operative Society, 1962)

Metcalf, W M, *A History of the County of Renfrew* (Paisley, 1905)

Murray, R, *History of the Barrhead Co-operative Society Limited, 1861–1911* (Barrhead Co-operative Society Ltd, 1911)

Murray, R, *Barrhead Co-operative Society* (Barrhead Co-operative Society Ltd, 1911)

Murray, R, *Barrhead Co-operative Society 1911–1936* (Barrhead Co-operative Society Ltd, 1937)

Pryde, D, *A History of the Parish of Neilston* (Paisley, 1910)

Ritchie, A (ed), *Govan and Its Early Medieval Sculpture* (Stroud, 1994)

Robertson, A J, 'Textiles', in A Slaven and S Checkland (eds), *Dictionary of Scottish Business Biography, 1860–1960, I: the staple industries* (Aberdeen, 1986)

Shands, G M, *Shanks & Co, Ltd, Barrhead. The First Hundred Years, 1851–1951* (np, nd)

Shaw, J, *Water Power in Scotland 1550–1870* (Edinburgh, 1984)

Slaven, A, *The Development of the West of Scotland: 1750–1960* (London, 1975)

Smith, R, *The Making of Scotland: a comprehensive guide to the growth of Scotland's cities, towns and villages* (Edinburgh, 2001)

Taylor, C, *The Levern Delineated in a Series of Views of the Most Interesting Scenery along the Banks & Vicinity: with historical and topographical sketches* (Glasgow, 1831)

Thomas, J, *A Regional History of the Railways of Great Britain, 6: Scotland The Lowlands and the Borders* (revised edn, Newton Abbott, 1984)

Turnbull, G J (ed), *A History of the Calico Printing Industry of Great Britain* (Altrincham, 1951)

Urquhart, R M, *The Burghs of Scotland and the Police of Towns Act 1850* (Scottish Library Association, Motherwell, 1989)

Further Scottish textile references are given on the following website:
www.scottishtextiles.org.uk
See also:
www.barrhead-scotland.com
www.scotland.gov.uk/News/Releases/2003/08/3966 21 July 2004

Cartographic sources

'Renfrewshire', by T Pont (*c* 1590s)

'Ainslie's map of the county of Renfrew', by J Ainslie (surveyed 1796, published 1800)

Map of Barrhead & Neilson, Ordnance Survey, (1863/64) Available: www.old-maps.co.uk

'Renfrewshire', Ordnance Survey, 1st edn, 1:2500 scale (sheet XII.15, 1857)

'Renfrewshire', Ordnance Survey, 2nd edn, 1:2500 scale (sheet XII.15, 1896)

Map of Roman Britain, Ordnance Survey, (4th edn, 1978)

Soil Survey of Scotland, *South-West Scotland Soil*, 1:250,000 scale, sheet 6 (Aberdeen, 1982)

Soil Survey of Scotland, *South-West Scotland Land Capability for Agriculture*, 1:250,000 scale, sheet 6 (Aberdeen, 1982)

Aerial photographs

Several series of aerial and oblique photographs of Barrhead and the surrounding area held by the Royal Commission on the Ancient and Historical Monuments of Scotland, 16 Bernard Terrace, Edinburgh.

Index

Entries in **bold** refer to the figures